Designi[illegible] Authori[illegible]g Experiences

Greg Dunlap

Editors: Lisa Maria Marquis, Frances Duncan, and Susan Bond
Design and production: Brenda Halvorson
Cover design: Jared Ponchot

ISBN: 979-8-9917629-0-8
Splash Hit Publishing
Poulsbo, WA

10 9 8 7 6 5 4 3 2 1

Table of Contents

For Hawkeye, Lyman, and Mimi.

Introduction

> "In my experience, the number one complaint of organizations looking to replace their CMS is, simply, 'our editors hate it.'"
>
> —Deane Barker, Real World Content Modeling
>
> *(https://deanebarker.net/books/real world-content-modeling/)*

At the 2020 edition of Confab, the premier conference for content strategy (RIP), Laura Robertson took the main stage and said she was going to take a poll. "Raise your hand if you love your content management system." The entire room went silent. (Okay, fine—I was the only one who raised their hand.)

Almost everyone hates their content management system (CMS). I rarely go a day without someone complaining to me about how awful their CMS is, how hard it is to use, or how it gets in the way of people who just want to do their job. And you know what? It's hard to argue with that. Forms that are clunky or slow, documentation that is impossible to understand (if it's present at all), content that is impossible to find—the laundry list of grievances is long, and in most cases, fully justified.

The thing is, people aren't really complaining about their CMS. They're complaining about custom functionality that doesn't fit with the way they work. They're complaining about opaque business requirements sent down from on high with no explanation or consideration for the people who enter content into the system. They're complaining about feeling disenfranchised from the system they're expected to use daily.

Too often in content projects, the needs of authors are barely taken into consideration. This can be incredibly frustrating for content authors and also for the business. Organizations may spend millions of dollars on web content management projects. With that kind of money on the line, you'd think they might focus on creating a system that people want to use, rather than one that fills them with dread. But that's not usually what happens. There are lots of reasons why the needs of authors are not considered, but this book is here to say: enough is enough.

In the pages that follow, you will find concrete strategies—for project teams of any size, budget, or level of technical know-how—to improve content authoring experiences and empower editorial teams to do their best work. Topics we'll cover include:

- Circumstances that impact the author experience, including organizational governance, workflow, and structured content.
- User research techniques that help you create an author experience to fit the way people work.
- Techniques to improve content entry and administration with well-designed forms, editor dashboards, and documentation that's helpful.
- Accessibility of the authoring interface, and how to encourage authors to create accessible content.
- Supporting and maintaining your systems after launch and into the future.

You may have picked up this book thinking you would find a set of rules to make any authoring experience the best it can be. Spoiler alert: there is no definitive best authoring experience. No one set of rules will make every web editor happier and more productive. There is only the best experience *for your organization* and its editors.

That means this is a "what" and "why" book, not a "how to" book. For example, I will discuss when it is and isn't appropriate to use required fields for content entry, but I won't talk about how you implement required fields in any systems. Since how to implement and change functionality in different content management systems varies widely, this is a topic that would be impossible to cover in the scope of this book. I also won't cover topics such as how to choose or install a content management system. Instead, I'll share principles anyone can use to improve the experience of their content authors, regardless of project specifics.

This book covers a wide variety of techniques to improve the content authoring experience, but not every activity we discuss will make sense for every project. I have used these approaches across many different projects but never all of them on any one project. Software projects are always limited by scope, budget, and deadlines. Take inspiration from the chapters that follow, and figure out what is most important and manageable in the work that you are doing.

By the time you're done with this book, you'll have learned how to improve the experience of content authors by using practical, scalable methods—and you'll understand why this work is crucial to the success of any web project.

I have made the screenshots, links, and resources used in this book available online for easier use. Feel free to visit *https://authoringexperience.com/resources* or scan the QR code to access them.

1. The Authoring Experience

When you create a piece of content in a content management system (CMS), you'll typically use a web form with fields that combine to create the page that site visitors see (**Fig 1.1**). The forms allow you to enter the information needed to create a piece of content. At its simplest, a content form has a title, body text with formatting options, images, and a way to categorize the content using tags or topics. Sometimes you can add metadata about the content—information that describes the article and its function but isn't displayed to the end user. Metadata includes information such as an article's URL string, and whether it's ready to be published.

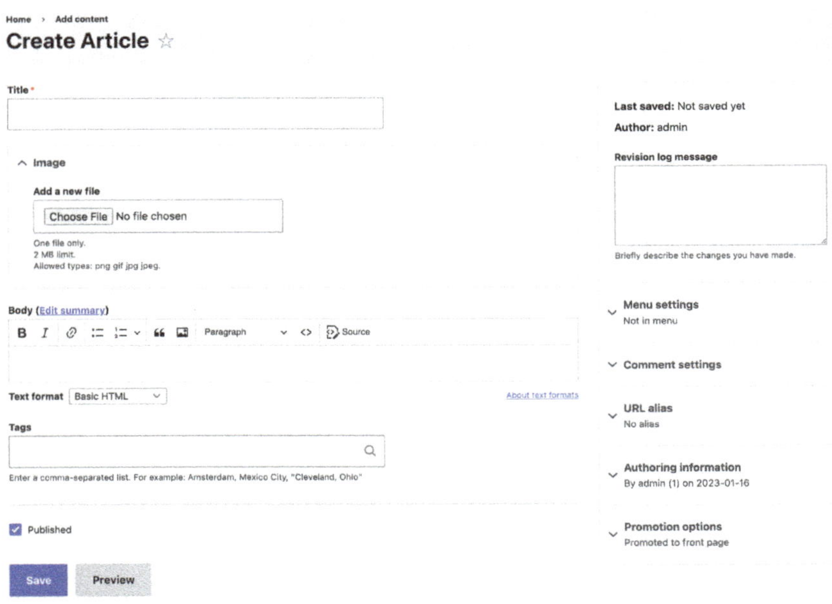

Fig 1.1: *This article creation screen is a simple example of content authoring. Content creation experiences are often much more complex, with dozens of fields and other elements.*

Content authors around the world fill out forms like this all the time. The process of using these forms is the central part of what we call the *authoring experience*. It seems simple. We throw some fields on a form. People fill them out. What's the problem?

But even a simple form has more depth than is immediately apparent. There are many questions you should consider when creating interfaces like this, including (but not limited to):

- What information needs to be captured?
- What fields are needed to capture that information?
- What interface or "widget" should each field have?
- What order are the fields laid out in?
- What information is initially available, and what is hidden?
- How and where is the hidden information accessed?
- What kind of help text is there to assist content authors?
- What fields are required to publish the content?
- What biases or assumptions did the person creating the form bring in with them?
- What accommodations are made to users with disabilities?

This list could go on, and this is just for a simple piece of content. Many content entry interfaces are more complex, encompassing more than a hundred fields spread across multiple tabs. Every time someone decides to add a field, move its position on the form, or make it required, they are impacting the authoring experience. More importantly, they impact the work of a real person who's trying to do their best in a system that often wasn't designed to meet their needs.

The authoring experience doesn't stop with forms but includes interactions such as moving content from one workflow state to another. Some systems involve complex interactions like the ability to drag and drop blocks of content to arrange them on a page. All of these contribute to—or detract from—a system's authoring experience.

Why is the authoring experience important?

Why does the authoring experience matter? What are the consequences of a clunky or unusable authoring experience? The answer is simple: a clean, usable, friendly authoring system produces better content. This happens for several reasons.

- **A CMS only works if people use it**. You want your users to enter and update content as needed. That's the whole point of the system. If authors dread using your system, they will find any excuse not to, and they'll rush through their work when they do. People might not look forward to using even the most well-designed system, but your organization will have a much better chance of success if your CMS users don't hate it.
- **A thoughtful authoring experience increases efficiency.** Making information easier to find, removing barriers to entering content, and reducing the number of steps all make the content creation process easier and faster. A full-time content author might work with content entry forms dozens of times a week. I've seen systems where a task such as adding an image requires up to ten steps, or where finding one piece of content is so arduous that the author uses Google instead. All of these interactions add up. They frustrate authors and waste time that your organization could better use to create or improve content.
- **An intentional authoring experience guides authors.** When an authoring experience is intentionally designed, it will guide your authors towards decisions that improve

content and away from decisions that make the content worse. You want to make the right things easy and the wrong things hard, not the other way around.

Throughout this book, we'll spend a lot of time looking at how to make things easier for site authors. However, making something *too* easy can come at the cost of good content. One example of this is text editor configuration. Many content management systems come with the ability to provide text formatting through an editing interface (**Fig 1.2**).

Fig 1.2: *A CMS text editor allows users to apply different formatting options to text, such as bold, italic, and bulleted lists.*

Most CMS text editors allow users to upload and embed an image. It's a simple task that most authors are familiar with, but it can introduce problems. Images can get placed in positions that cause the text to flow weirdly. Or authors get that part right but don't test on mobile, and the text gets messed up on different screen sizes. Or, they upload a low-resolution image and make it larger, resulting in an image that's pixelated. Authors love the simplicity of image embed functionality, but embedding can have a negative impact on the end user's experience. Solutions for managing this can be burdensome for authors, requiring more steps or removing flexibility. Finding the right balance is key—and we'll talk about this more in the next chapter.

A thoughtfully designed authoring experience produces better content, and better content is good for business. But beyond the business case for improving the authoring experience, there is a human reason. We shouldn't design systems that make people miserable. Authors may use a CMS over very long periods of time, when even the smallest pain points can add up. Content authors are human, and our professional lives are intertwined with theirs because we build these systems for them to use.

Before we talk more about the "what" and "why" of authoring experiences, it will help to get an idea of how we got here and learn why these systems work the way they do. Let's take a step back and dig into how the modern CMS came into being.

A brief history of web content authoring

The World Wide Web is based on a markup language called HTML, which takes the text on a page and adds contextual information like "This bit is bold" or "Put an image here." In the early days of the web, HTML was stored in static files—text documents sitting in a folder on a server. Every web page was a file, and to change the content on a page you had to get the file from the server, edit the HTML, and put the changed file back.

HTML is fairly simple (or at least it was at the time), but a decent amount of technical knowledge was required to make changes to a website. You had to make sure that nobody was making changes to the same file as you at the same time—otherwise somebody's work was going to get overwritten. Moving files required arcane command line tools and an understanding of file systems and permissions. At that point, most websites didn't really have anyone "in charge." Oversight of an organization's website fell to whatever random, tech-savvy folks happened to be ahead of the curve and whoever wanted to take it on. Changes tended to be simple, and when they needed to be made, the knowledgeable people made them. (In some cases the website people just did whatever they wanted because the organization barely knew the web existed.)

By the late 1990s, this model started to fall apart. As sites became more complex and mission critical, leaders in marketing and sales needed more control over their content. They bristled at the idea of having to run everything through whoever happened to be running the website in addition to doing their main job. Applications like Microsoft FrontPage started to bridge the gap by demystifying HTML and providing a visual interface for building pages.

But what was really needed was a way to break the content from the HTML files that contained it—a content management system. There were few off-the-shelf systems like this at the time, so many organizations built their own. Some early content management systems were little more than a text area where you could type HTML to be replicated on the site (**Fig 1.3**). As time went on, these systems became more fully featured.

Fig 1.3: *This is the first content management system I ever built. You could create and edit blocks of HTML, which a developer would place in specific areas on a site. The first version didn't even have a visual editor.*

The introduction of content management wasn't just a technical change—it was also an organizational one. As content management systems matured, responsibility for the website moved away from those with HTML knowledge. Now, a broader range of people were empowered to own an organization's digital content.

This was the beginning of a switch: as the tools became more approachable and less specialized, the content became less approachable and more specialized. More planning was needed to create content in large organizations, and since the content was imperative to success, it required more care.

As the needs of organizations grew during the late 1990s to early 2000s, off-the-shelf content management systems entered the scene, along with a market of consultants to customize them. Some systems were commercial products from big names like Adobe, and some were open-source upstarts like Drupal and WordPress. Over time, these products improved until they could be used without extensive training.

As content management systems became easier to use, the web got more and more complicated. Mobile phones and responsive web design rose in prominence. Content needed to be reused on other websites and mobile applications. Managing metadata for devices other than the human eye became essential, especially as organizations began to prioritize accessibility and SEO.

These changes required structured content. Understanding the individual elements of a page is crucial for creating layouts for various screen sizes and devices. Let's say you have a photo and a piece of text. This isn't enough information to know where they should go on the page. But if you know that you have a product photo and a customer testimonial, you can make good decisions. A CMS that offers semantic page structure is a very different authoring experience than one where you type and upload photos into an HTML field.

I hear lots of people talk about how their CMS is hard to use, and yet content management systems are easier to use than they have ever been. It's the *content* that's become more complex. As the people who are building these systems, we are responsible for representing that complexity in a way that authors will be able to understand. This is one of the biggest challenges in modern content management.

Sometimes I wonder if we should move back toward a world of specialized content authors, or at least authors with an understanding of how the web works. Not an HTML expert, but someone who looks at site content holistically. Someone who can address content with an eye toward their organization's goals and priorities. Unfortunately, many companies think of content authoring as something anyone can do with a low level of training—someone just dumping words onto a website on the side while they do their "real" job.

You know what does not make for a good authoring experience? Putting uprepared people in front of a tool that wasn't designed for them, and expecting them to be successful.

Authors are users

Content authors are users of your website, just like the people who browse your website from the comfort of their homes. We can't make the modern web any less complicated, and we can't force companies to take content seriously and properly hire and train the people who create it. What we *can* do is understand the forces that contribute to a content management experience, consider users' needs, and improve the systems we create—as well as our content authors' working lives.

One of those forces is CMS architecture: how content is structured and presented within the system. CMS design decisions have lasting impacts on authors, often in non-obvious ways. The balance between content structure and presentational flexibility is one of the defining forces that drives the authoring experience. In the next chapter, we'll explore how different systems strike this balance, and how each kind affects the authoring experience.

2. **Structure vs. Flexibility**

As we saw in the previous chapter, the changing demands of the web required structured content. In content management systems, this manifested as a shift away from simple interfaces, like an HTML editor, toward forms where the individual properties of a piece of content were represented as fields, each of which had to be filled out individually. This move enabled a lot of necessary functionality on the web, but it came at a cost. Authors couldn't copy and paste a Word document, drop in a couple photos, and press save. It took more time to create content, required more attention to ensure it was created correctly, and removed a lot of control over page presentation from authors.

This tension between structure and flexibility is the most common issue I encounter when working with authors. Authors want freedom and ease of use, and organizations need structure to enable vital functionality. In this chapter, we'll dive deeper into the importance of structured content, as well as the pros and cons of different kinds of content structures and what you can do to find the balance between authors' needs and organizational priorities.

More than words

Structure turns content from words and images to data that can be understood by a machine—a CMS, search engines, AI bots, RSS feeds, and more. Adding structure gives semantic meaning to the individual content components on a page. We decide on content structure in a process called content modeling. This is done by determining what kind of content you have (press release, event, news, etc.) and then defining the individual pieces that make up the content (author, headshot, date, location, etc.). Once you know what everything on the page really is—beyond photos and videos and blocks of text—then you understand its purpose and meaning, and you can place it in the right context. Structured content separates the information on the page from its visual presentation.

Let's say you need to create a blog post. In a very simple content management system, you might enter a title first, and then in the body, put the date of the post and the author. Maybe you even upload a headshot of the author. Great! Now you have a blog post. You managed some content (**Fig 2.1**)!

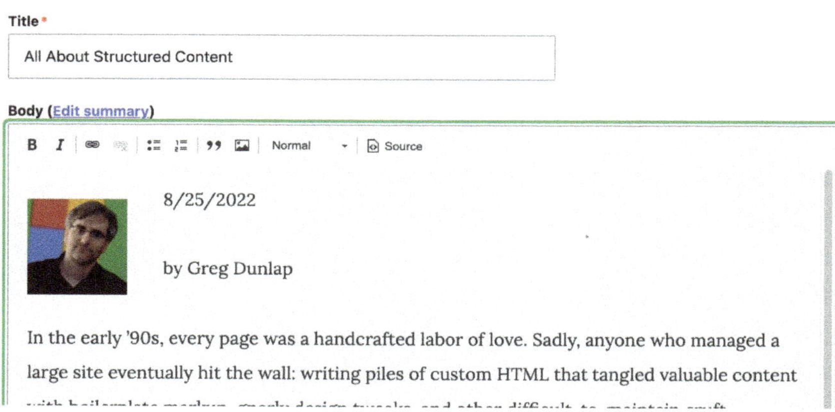

Fig 2.1: *This simple CMS allows an author to create a basic layout with their content, but there is no way they can associate any meaningful data with individual pieces like the date, author's name, or headshot.*

Unfortunately, this method has several problems.

- Author and date information may not be displayed in the same place from post to post. They'll only be as consistent as the content author who creates them.

- No one can find, sort, or filter posts, based on who wrote them or when they were published, because the system doesn't recognize there's an author or a date in this blob of words.
- The system can't make decisions on how to display blog posts based on the content's meaning, so the display won't be responsive to a change in device or orientation. You may want to hide the author headshot on mobile to create more room for people to read the post. That's impossible here, because the system only knows there is a photo. It doesn't know the photo's meaning or purpose.
- This content isn't accessible to people using assistive technology. There's no way to provide added context to the author or date information, and there may be no way to do so for the headshot either.

So what if we instead split out the date and author information from the main body of the post and provided data that could identify those to the system and to site users (**Fig 2.2**)?

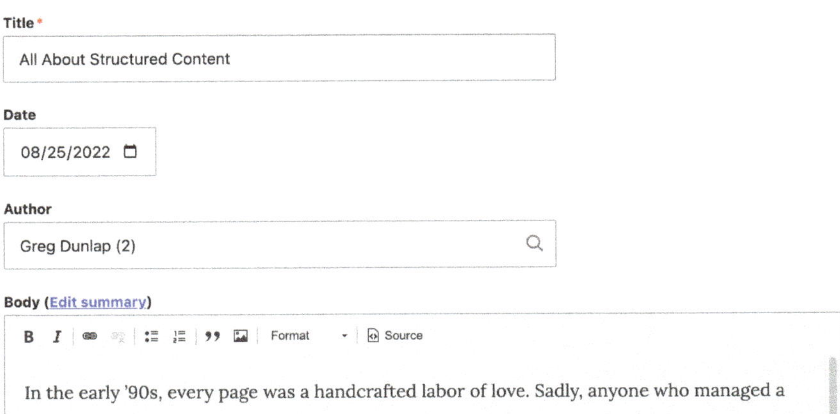

Fig 2.2: *By breaking the author and date into discrete fields, the system can now add contextual data to enable necessary functionality.*

Now we have a blog post that solves the problems we laid out previously:

- Authors and dates can be presented consistently across all blog posts, because the system can identify and style them appropriately.
- Site visitors and content editors can find, sort, and filter posts based on author or date.
- Page display can adjust responsively, based on the needs of any device.
- Posts are accessible to people using assistive tech because they include the necessary context.

Structured content is more than just words. Structure gives context to the words, images, and other types of content on a web page, and the system uses this context to create a modern web experience for all users.

When structure causes problems

Structured content can make the authoring experience feel complicated. Authors see field-based interfaces with their smaller chunks of content, and they can feel overwhelmed. Using them is not as simple as pasting text into a big body field.

Site authors also feel constrained by structure. They want more control over the appearance of the content they create. They find the templates too restrictive and want to flex their creative muscles. These are some of the considerations that make tools like WordPress so popular. The classic authoring experience in WordPress is an interface where content authors can do practically anything. When they lose this control, they feel like they've been demoted. A part of what they considered their work is taken away from them.

I've encountered well-trained content authors who understand structured content and welcome it—but not often. Organizations experiencing the most trouble with structured content authoring tend to exhibit the same three qualities:

- **Poorly trained authors.** Those who aren't trained in the CMS and who don't understand the importance of structured content will prefer a simpler interface.
- **Part-time authors.** Those who are experts in topics other than the web, or who work in the system as only a small part of their job, will have less time for content entry and will focus less on content quality. Their motivation is to get the content on the site quickly so they can move on to their primary responsibilities.
- **Low content maturity.** A high content maturity organization has a plan for what content they create, when they create it, and for what purpose. A low content maturity organization has no plan and as a result can have authors who prioritize the wrong things.

When the greater organization doesn't value or even understand content work, it's harder for authors to understand what content types are for, or how to organize them.

Building pages

Your content management system and individual content types can handle different degrees of structure, depending on what your content needs.

Some content adapts well to structure. Events require distinct properties: start date, end date, location, hours, cost, and so on. Each property is its own field with individual attributes. A structured content type like this is easy to present consistently so site visitors can find event information. (**Fig 2.3**).

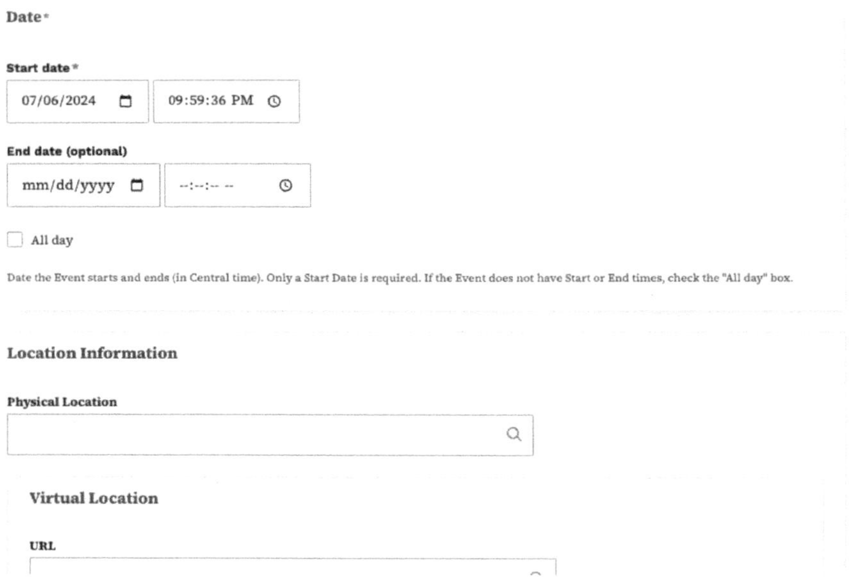

Fig 2.3: *A small section of the authoring interface for an event. Every piece of information needed to construct the event has its own distinct field. The entire interface is much longer and includes fields for photos, registration links, name of the primary contact, and more.*

On the other end of the spectrum, something like a press release doesn't call for that much structure. The primary content is the text of the press release. You need a field for that, sure, but the field contains running text and that's it. Maybe you add a couple fields for contact information and a release date. But the main thing people are concerned with is that block of text, which has no inherent structural qualities that carry through from press release to press release.

Those extremes present easy solutions, but there is *a lot* of content in the gooey space between them.

Over the years, content management systems have tried to bridge that gap.

Page builders

Recently, the *prevailing solution* has been page builders. Page builders are interfaces where authors use click-and-drag functionality to build content pages. They enter content into components and place them on pages they've created for their specific needs. Page building systems support layout flexibility with some level of design consistency.

Page builders rose in popularity with tools like Squarespace and Wix. Over time, most content management systems added this functionality. Some systems went all in on page building, ignoring any other ways to interact with content (**Fig 2.4**).

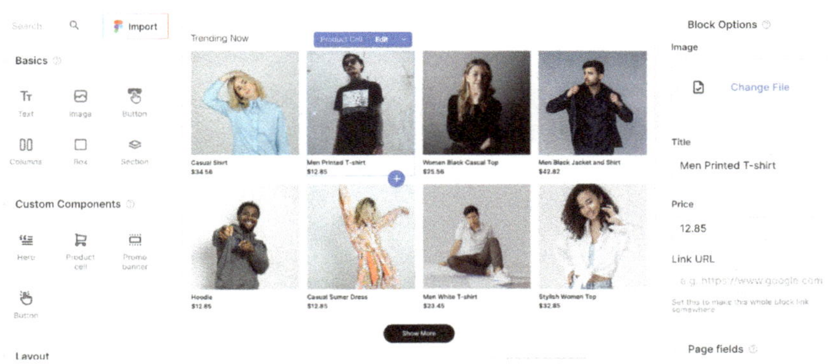

Fig 2.4: *A small sample of a page-building interface. The left panel shows components to add, the middle allows draggable organizing, and the right, data for each individual component can be entered in its fields.*

Organizations often start using page builders for good reasons, like for their weird quarterly campaign landing pages, which are customized from season to season but still need some sense of order. Where they get into trouble is when authors use page builders for more and more use cases, even when the content doesn't need this flexibility. Pages become inconsistent, and the meaning of the content is lost. It's harder to tell events from articles from landing pages, causing problems with findability, site organization, listings, and a host of other issues.

Block-based editors

Another common solution, block-based editors are an expansion of the traditional HTML editor that combines a body field with the functionality of a page builder. There's an open body text field, to which authors can add components or blocks of other content. The website Medium pioneered his kind of editing experience, followed more recently by the WordPress Gutenberg editor (**Fig 2.5**). Systems often use block-based editors when content is mostly textual, like long-form articles and information pages. In these cases, text is the primary content, and flexibility around page layout and design are less important.

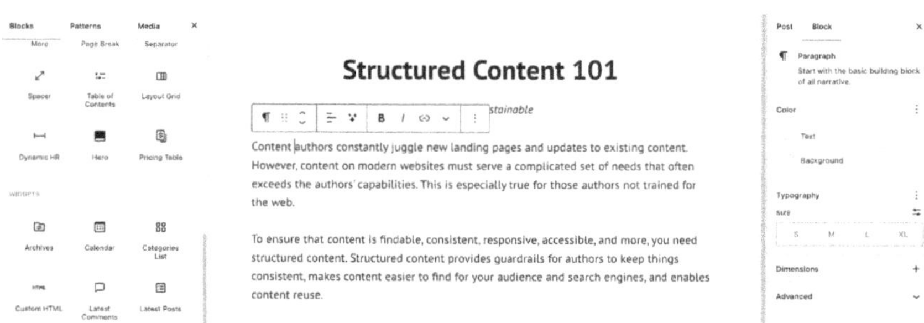

Fig 2.5: *The WordPress Gutenberg editor, an example of a block-based editing experience. This is similar to the page-building experience but more focused on the flow of text.*

Which option is best for your authors?

How to choose

Why not give the authors what they want? This is a book about the authoring experience. If the best experience is a page builder, then what's the problem?

The problem is that unless designed very carefully, page builders and block-based editors remove the content's semantic meaning. They focus on how the content looks rather than what it means, reducing the benefits of structured content.

Let's look at a common component through a page-building lens. Many systems contain a component that consists of a headline, a block of text, a photo, and a link. These are intended to bring attention to specific content and drive users further into a site. They go by different names, but let's call this one a *promo* (**Fig 2.6**). The promo seems very simple and flexible, but it has no meaning. Does it link to a featured article? Does the call to action generate a lead? Does it highlight a new product or an announcement? There's no way to tell without analyzing the content. At some point, someone will wish they *could* tell, because the lack of clarity will affect the content's presentation, or the content might not repurpose clearly throughout the site or migrate well to a new system down the road.

Fig 2.6: *A promo component. While this example is a call to action, a promo component often gets repurposed for many things throughout a website, robbing it of any semantic meaning.*

OK then, let's add more structure and forget about flexibility. Holding this hard line will alienate content authors and drive a wedge between them and the people designing and implementing the CMS. By now, some of you are probably screaming about how authors should fill out the information and stop worrying about presentation. You are correct in principle—but this is not the reality in most organizations. We in the development and strategy world are very concerned with how content is structured, but many authors are more concerned with how it looks. That's not changing anytime soon. To improve content for everyone, we need to find a balance between our academic principles and authors' real-world ones.

The challenge is for everyone to stop thinking about tools as the primary driver for decision-making. Instead, start with your content. Figure out what the content needs, and apply the right tool. To do that, let's look at three different kinds of content structure, their inherent properties, and what works best for each.

Highly structured content

This type of content has:

- Rigid structure and fields
- A display that's controlled by the CMS
- Little to no design flexibility

Highly structured content has distinct properties that are consistent from page to page. Events, locations, and people are all highly structured. Let's say your authors manage content about stores where customers buy your product. Each store has an address, a phone number, hours of operation, and other details. You'll need to break down these attributes into several known and predictable fields, and design content types around them.

Consistent display of this kind of content makes it easy for users to find the information they need. Similar content should have a similar look and feel.

For highly structured content, the CMS should provide a high level of control and a low level of flexibility. A traditional, fielded interface is a good choice here. It allows you to control each property individually and to standardize how it's displayed. Predictable fields also make the content easier to query and list—for both users on the front end and authors on the back end.

Textual content

This type of content has:

- Some structure, especially for textual elements (headers, lists, quotes, etc.)
- A display that's mostly controlled by the CMS

- Some design flexibility, with components embedded in text areas with few restrictions on their placement

Content types such as articles, press releases, and informational pages are all textual. They're made up of words meant to be read from beginning to end, with some additional elements, such as imagery, pull quotes, and other bits that expand on the content and draw people in.

Traditionally, authors have created textual content using a rich text field with a visual editor. This is still a common solution and one I use frequently. Before you implement any solution, get to know the content so you make sure to offer appropriate editing options that will support it. A magazine article might need options for an image gallery or video embeds, while a press release might not need any formatting options at all. Block-based editors can be a good option for textual content, with the same caveats—provide the functionality that the content requires. Don't throw the kitchen sink at it.

Marketing content

This type of content has:

- A total lack of structure, or a partially structured container holding adjustable, structured components
- A display that's controlled by the author
- Full design flexibility

Marketing content is best served by design flexibility. Examples include campaign landing pages, site home pages, and main navigation landing pages. These pages don't contain primary content. Their purpose is to drive users to primary content deeper in the site. Marketing content may be ephemeral and change with shifting priorities, seasons, or sales. Or it may be tied to a campaign or upcoming event. Marketing content benefits from a bespoke design treatment so it will stand out from the rest of the site. But it's modular, not *completely unstructured*, and so it requires some structure for all the reasons outlined above, especially findability and responsiveness.

A CMS with page-building capabilities is valuable for marketing content. Combined with a set of semantically structured components, you get the benefits of structured content and the ability to create differing layouts and design treatments.

However, most content isn't this cut and dried. We often find ourselves in situations where textual content is supported by highly structured content, and we need to solve for both cases in one content type. These guidelines will serve as a good starting point when you're exploring the kinds of tools you want to offer to your authors. The most important thing is to use the right tools for the right purposes—and also, to enforce guardrails to prevent tools from being used for the wrong purposes.

Structure and flexibility in the real world

Several years ago I worked on a large project for a state government. They were building a system to support their agencies, whose primary content was text-heavy informational pages, with a secondary need for topical landing pages and flexible home pages. As part of the discovery process, our team interviewed project stakeholders and content authors at the agencies (more on this later when we talk about research). Content maturity was low across the agencies. While there were some exceptions, most of the agencies' authors were subject matter experts with little web content experience. For many, using the CMS was only a small part of their job.

One refrain our team heard over and over was that authors wanted more flexibility in page design. They wanted a full rich-text editor with source control. When we pressed them, asking what goals they were trying to achieve with that flexibility, they didn't have anything specific. The most common answer was that the pages were "a wall of text" and they wanted to make them visually interesting.

We built templates using a robust visual editor, with strict image placement options and a way to embed teasers to other content. Authors struggled with the new system at first, but after a short adjustment period they preferred it to a full-featured rich text editor. It turned out authors didn't want total control over the page, they wanted better options to add headers, lists, and other elements to break it up.

We weren't always so successful, though. We also made a page builder for creating flexible landing pages with re-usable components. Each component had design options, like orienting an image on the left or right, or styling the component as a card with an icon. Some of these options were global, so a change in one placement of a component would change it in all placements. Other options were per-instance, so a change would affect only that placement, while the others stayed the same. We thought this level of flexibility would empower authors and help them take advantage of content reusability. Instead, they found it confusing. They could never keep track of which options were global and which weren't, and whenever they expected one, it would invariably be the other. Eventually they became reluctant to do *anything*. This was the exact opposite of what we'd hoped to achieve.

We'd offered to remove this functionality, but that would have required a lot of manual updating by the authors, or updating all of the different implementations in a way that didn't mess up existing designs. So it's still there.

Removing flexibility is *always* harder than adding it. We hadn't tested the reusable components feature with the authors before rolling it out, and that had come back to bite us. We also overestimated our authors' ability to work with complex functionality. We knew from our initial research that the author pool wasn't very experienced, but we had some large agencies that had needed complex functionality. Finding that balance had proven to be a challenge.

Finding the balance

Authors will always ask for more flexibility. Before you write a blank check, ask:

- What are your content goals?
- What does the content need, and how does the CMS support or impede that need?
- How comfortable are your authors, when it comes to dealing with complexity?

Explore where these questions intersect and find a balance.

Structure and flexibility are often presented as an either/or choice that leads to an antagonistic relationship between site authors and web-development professionals. Yes, you need structure to create modern, accessible, and mobile-friendly websites. You also need to meet authors where they are and give them tools to balance that structure with the flexibility they desire to meet their content goals.

To make balanced decisions, you need to know the circumstances outside the CMS: your project *context*. What type of organization are you working with, and who are your content authors? That's what we're going to look at in the next two chapters.

3. **Understanding Your Organization**

All content managements systems have a default, or out-of-the-box, authoring experience. These interfaces are not actually designed for anyone but are designed for "everyone." Their features are broadly applicable to many generic situations without being targeted to any specific ones. They're adequate for creating simple content, and they're awkward for anything else.

A good authoring experience is designed for the organization and authors who use it. To design for your environment, you need to understand your content in the context of your organization. In this chapter we will look at different organizational qualities and how they intersect to create differing CMS needs. These scenarios can be hard to see when you're mired in your project, but they'll highlight how the nature of your organization influences your authoring experience design and priorities.

Organizational characteristics

When I design a CMS, I always ask clients a few standard questions. Often the questions are technical, like "How much content do you have?" or "What external systems do you integrate with?" Answers to these questions require some digging, but they are usually easy to get.

I also ask about their organization. Organizational questions are ones like "What kind of authors do you have?" or "What is your content governance process?" These answers are harder to get. Usually, the company has been so focused on getting the development effort started that they haven't stopped to think about any of this. And yet, the answers to these questions can completely change the solutions I recommend.

Say you have one client whose authors are well-trained content professionals, and another client whose authors are academics who update the organization's website in their spare time. This one difference will change the tools we might build in major ways—and that's just one variable among many. Let's look at some of the organizational characteristics that influence the authoring experience.

Business model

Is your organization a for-profit company whose website is used to sell products? Or are you a not-for-profit, focused on messaging and motivating people to donate and volunteer? Or are you in the public sector with the goal of providing information to your constituents?

Different business models have differing content needs. This impacts the content design and the authoring experience of those who are putting the content into the system. A product-driven company will want to ensure their content cross-references products and creates calls-to-action to push users through the sales funnel. On the other hand, a public-sector site will focus on clear, understandable information with little fuss in the context of a single page.

Industry

Imagine two commerce-centric organizations with active, tightly planned publishing schedules. One is in a highly regulated industry, and the other is not. The organization in the regulated industry is likely to have a complicated publishing workflow, involving sign-off from a legal team before anything can go live. Meanwhile, the organization in the consumer space can have a simpler, more agile workflow, putting more freedom in the hands of the authors. Which organization is more like yours?

Content authors

Who is your authoring team? Is it large and distributed, or small and tightly integrated? Is it divided into teams by function, or subject, or is everyone together in one group? Are your authors skilled in web content management, or are they subject matter experts with little CMS experience?

Small, experienced teams can use complex, flexible interfaces. Less experienced teams need a system that's easier to understand and use.

Publishing schedule

How often are you creating and publishing content? Is it a constant, carefully planned stream, or is it ad hoc?

An active, formal production schedule requires support features, like an editorial calendar, or visualizations of evolving content workflow states. Some organizations also need scheduled publishing tools, so they can publish and unpublished automatically at set times.

Editorial workflow

What process needs to be in place to move your content from draft to publication? Do formal approvals happen before content goes live, or can most people publish anything once they feel it's ready—or something in between? How do roles differ? Who can create content, and who can publish it?

Workflow adds complexity. A successful one requires tools such as dashboards, where authors can see what content needs their attention. Workflow can be further complicated by factors such as publishing schedules and author skills.

Content governance

Who owns your CMS platform? Who oversees your content? Is there a style guide? Who makes decisions about what content is published and when? Is content managed by authors or by a separate team? Is it a publishing free-for-all?

Content governance is a set of guidelines and policies that dictates how an organization creates, manages, and publishes content. Your organization's governance model can either support or exacerbate all the issues we've discussed so far.

Content maturity

Content maturity refers to the extent to which an organization's content is driven by strategic planning and decision making. An organization with low content maturity creates content in a disorganized or haphazard way. Individual writers create content how and when they want, with little relation to organizational strategy or goals.

At the other end of the spectrum, an organization with high content maturity operates like a well-oiled machine. All content ties directly to established goals and priorities, regardless of who writes it. Analytics and research drive content production in measurable and repeatable ways.

Now that you have a basic understanding of different organizational characteristics, let's look at some examples and their impact on the authoring experience.

Intersections

An organization's characteristics often influence one another and combine in different ways. They don't live in a vacuum—they're intersectional, and changing even one of these characteristics can drastically affect the solutions you provide for content authors. I recently worked with two state government clients whose projects looked almost identical on paper. However, one client was coming from a much higher level of content maturity than the other, and this single difference cascaded throughout the entire project, requiring completely different solutions.

Let's look at some common combinations of characteristics, to get a better idea of how different organizations need different types of authoring experiences.

Enterprise product

LFS Enterprises is a 1,000+ employee company that produces apps and sells products directly to consumers. They use their website to promote products and upcoming events such as webinars and conferences. Their primary focus is to educate prospective buyers and generate leads, with a secondary focus on supporting existing customers by providing a knowledge base, tips-and-tricks blog posts, and support forums.

- **Organization type**: For-profit, large scale, product.
- **Authors**: Content specialists, hired for their writing and editing skills, who understand SEO, analytics, and accessibility. A large author pool is well staffed to meet their demanding market.
- **Publishing schedule**: Very frequent. New content and updates go out every day.

- **Workflow**: Simple. Authors can publish blog and event posts after a basic review. High-profile product marketing pages require more oversight, with several levels of review and approval.
- **Content governance**: Sits with the product content teams, coordinated with marketing and product. As each product has grown, teams spend more time focused on their own needs and less time collaborating with other teams or thinking strategically. Attempts to change this have been met with resistance or apathy.
- **Content maturity**: High

Authoring experience impact

With such a large volume of content being published every day, content authors need configurable dashboards to track their work. Notifications remind them of content they might have forgotten about or that needs to be reviewed. Product marketing pages require built-in workflow and preview tools, including those that allow page review for stakeholders without CMS logins. The content entry interface should get out of the way of authors, who will have many pieces in progress at different levels of completion, while still ensuring that metadata and categorization is in place before publication. Content authors have a deep understanding of CMS tools and have the skills to use them. However, team silos mean that implementing standards is difficult, because each team's style and governance differ.

Startup

Strap-a-Rocket is a fast-growing product software startup with 150 employees, and they're adding more every day. Small and scrappy, they sell two products directly from their website.

- **Organization type**: For-profit, small scale, product. Focused on lead generation and conversion.
- **Authors**: A mix of marketing specialists and content specialists. The company is growing explosively, and hiring has been a challenge, so everyone is slammed. People wear several hats and almost anyone might need to jump into the CMS to help as needed.
- **Publishing schedule**: Frequent. New content and updates going out all the time.
- **Workflow**: Very simple. Getting content out the door is prioritized over heavy review, except for some high-level marketing pages. Process takes a back seat to production.
- **Content governance**: Split between content and marketing teams. As the company grows, it has been hard to get any meaningful governance in place. These two teams, like the company itself, are still finding their way.
- **Content maturity**: Medium

Authoring experience impact

Content needs change frequently as the company continually pivots to try new sales techniques. As a result, their content—which supports marketing pillars, products, and case studies—changes often. The organization values their ability to swiftly make updates and get them published. To attract customers and convert leads, they must understand their SEO and analytics data. The content team is still trying to find the balance between "standardize operations" and "move fast and break things." Designing an authoring experience in this environment will be a challenge because the future is uncertain. Prioritize flexibility and know that change is inevitable.

Healthcare

Doctor Mario is a 1,000+ employee healthcare company focused on providing services to people who live in their service area. The company's website hosts educational materials about healthcare and common health issues, as well as information about how to access and pay for services. Their primary focus is on creating a smooth client service process, with a secondary focus on education and providing news on health topics.

- **Organization type**: For-profit, large scale.
- **Authors**: Subject matter experts with some basic knowledge of the web.
- **Publishing schedule**: Varies. Blog posts and news items are published frequently; large-scale initiatives less often. Authors sometimes contend with breaking news and fast-moving health situations.
- **Workflow**: Content is strictly controlled. Medical information goes through a detailed review process involving multiple rounds of review by the legal team.
- **Content governance**: Very siloed. Subject matter experts are reluctant to give up control of their areas.
- **Content maturity**: Medium to low

Authoring experience impact

The team's workflow needs are complex. Content moves through many different stages of approvals, and authors and approvers need to know their responsibilities. Most of the site content is long-form text. For this kind of content, does it make sense to build an approval process into the CMS, or should they use an external tool? Custom dashboards will help authors better track their work. CMS tools should encourage authors to create accessible, understandable content.

Media

Chef Yum Yum is a 1,000+ employee media company, providing multimedia content to a massive user base. The content crosses a variety of subject areas, including news, education, and entertainment. Their product is the content, sold actively through subscriptions or passively through advertising. Chef Yum Yum has invested in building tools and training staff to support and promote their product. Their authors and software are prepared to jump on any breaking story and change course accordingly.

- **Organization type**: For-profit, large scale
- **Authors**: Well-trained content professionals with a solid understanding of the web and topics like SEO and analytics.
- **Publishing schedule**: Constant. New content is always being prepared, going live, or being edited after going live.
- **Workflow**: Several stages of approval, mostly within the team. Outside teams, like legal, are rarely involved.
- **Content governance**: Situated in the product teams for the various divisions. Content production is well controlled and predictable, with schedules and plans available to everyone. Some production is automated through integration with external systems.
- **Content maturity**: High

Authoring experience impact

Content is the product, and this company takes it seriously. Their investment in technology and people reflects that. Their tools are more complex, to better manage extensive media and metadata. They hire experienced content authors and train them well. Author support continues after onboarding with continuing education and internal communities of practice. This company's content is highly structured into many different fields, some of which are conditional to field values elsewhere. These dependencies make it difficult to manage content in an external tool. The system needs workflows, with the same kinds of dashboards and process tools discussed in the healthcare example.

State government

A state government organization provides informational content to its constituencies. Technology adoption is very conservative, with a priority on stability. They have been slow to adapt to the web, and many content workflows center on uploading and managing PDFs. In some state governments, a central team manages a common CMS platform, but just as often, each agency runs their own independent site. Content production is done at the agency level, and the agencies have markedly different content needs. Keeping everyone happy is a challenge.

- **Organization type**: Public sector, large scale.
- **Authors**: Inconsistent. Some agencies have large, well-staffed teams. Other agencies have one person who spends a few hours on the website every week or two. Longer tenured employees may have web content management added to their workload even when they have no web content background. Web experience and engagement vary dramatically from agency to agency, but in general, content authors are subject matter experts with minimal web experience.
- **Publishing schedule**: Depends on the agency. Some are constant, some don't update content for weeks.
- **Workflow**: Light. Some agencies have fully thought-out workflows, but they are an edge case.

- **Content governance**: All content is produced at the agency level, so quality and consistency vary. If there is a central team managing the CMS, they may attempt to establish standards, but it's difficult to enforce them in a distributed governance model with no direct control over content.
- **Content maturity**: Low

Authoring experience impact

Diverse content needs and inexperienced authors make it a challenge to develop a system that works for everyone. And without strict governance, implementing consistent standards is tough. Authoring tools must focus on usability: make doing the right things easy and doing the wrong things hard. Document management is a big topic, due to the preponderance of PDFs. Enabling the functionality that authors need may add steps or new fields to the process. This doesn't usually go over well because it means more work, and authors don't always understand or appreciate the tradeoffs. Government entities tend to overlook ongoing author support and education.

Who are you?

Digging into your organization's structure and governance requires asking a lot of hard questions, but it's worth it. Understanding your organization, its content authors, and its publishing needs is how you design a system that will work for everyone. Gathering this information in advance will save you time and money, and give you a better chance of success.

Now that you know more about your organization, it's time to understand your authors a little better. Who are they? What kind of content do they create? What pain points do they encounter in your CMS? The answers won't be the same for every organization or system. There's only one way to find out the right answers for *your* project—and that means doing some research.

4. Understanding Your Authors

Authors are users of your system. Getting their input is as important to a project's success as getting input from end users. Many organizations do user research to determine what customers want and need. You can use the same techniques with internal users—content authors and editors. Using insights gained from research, you will be better able to build a system that makes it easy for authors to create the content their audience needs.

There are a couple of important goals to keep in mind when you're doing research with content authors: get authors invested, and understand their context.

Conducting research offers you an opportunity to connect with authors and get them invested in the content they create. In many organizations, there is distrust or even antagonism between content managers and the people who run the CMS. Bridging that gap can be difficult, but listening to authors who have probably never been asked for their opinions—and giving them a seat at the table with other stakeholders—can be the first step.

Research can also help you identify the different contexts in which people use the system. Do different roles perform different tasks? What gaps exist between functionality for new users and functionality for experienced ones? Identify these contexts and use cases so that you can design towards them later. Author research should happen early on, because the deeper you get into a project, the harder it is to change based on feedback.

There are lots of user research techniques. We can't cover them all here, but a few of the most helpful ones are surveys, in-person interviews, and workshops. Let's look at each more closely.

Surveys

> "In tort law the attractive nuisance doctrine refers to a hazardous object likely to attract those who are unable to appreciate the risk posed by the object. In the world of design research, surveys can be just such a nuisance."
>
> —Erika Hall, Just Enough Research (*https://abookapart.com/products/just-enough-research*)

Surveys can be terrible. Too often they are hastily put together and their substandard results are used to make decisions involving millions of dollars. Talking to people directly is the best way to get insights. If your pool of content authors is under a dozen, surveys aren't going to add to your tool kit.

However, many organizations have several hundred content authors, and directly interviewing them all is not realistic. In these cases, surveys can be a useful tool. Surveys don't replace other methods of research, but they can help identify trends that you can use to guide focused research later.

I usually survey content authors with two goals in mind:

- Identify trends and hot button topics to drill into when you do those interviews.
- Identify users to target for one-on-one interviews. They could be users who have interesting insights, strong passion, or a deep understanding of how organizational realities affect their work.

Given these goals, you'll want to design a survey that will give you useful information without being too overwhelming. Use a mix of closed and open-ended questions, focusing on the authors' experiences with their current system. The survey should be short enough for people to complete in five minutes. Resist the temptation to turn it into a fishing expedition, and instead focus on what you need to learn to move you forward.

Here are sample questions to ask your survey respondents:

- **What is your name and title?** Anonymous surveys can help people speak freely. But one of the benefits of running a survey is to find people to follow up with. You can't do that unless you know who they are. If you can you keep responses confidential and anonymous when you communicate with project stakeholders, then include this question in your survey. Provide an option to opt out of further contact for those who don't wish to be interviewed.
- **How much of your role involves editing or creating content on your website?** (Scale from 1 to 10 representing 10% to 100% of their time.) This helps establish author types and their roles. How many people work on content full time, part time, or on the side?
- **How often do you edit or add content on the site?** (Range from once a week or less to multiple times a day.) Similar to the above question, but this will help you understand the production flow.
- **How difficult do you find the following content tasks?** The answers to this question usually include content stages: choosing a content type, adding images or documents, content entry, following a style guide, etc. Provide a five-step response range, from very easy to very difficult.

- **How time consuming are the following content tasks?** Some tasks are very time consuming but easy. The response to this question should use the same list of tasks (content stages) as the previous one, so you can compare across the two. Note where the two diverge, to help you discover what users are struggling with.

These last two open-ended questions focus on the author's experiences. This is the place where they will have the most to say, because it's their lived reality.

- **What are your biggest pain points when using the system?** What does everyone hate? What gets in their way every single day?
- **What functionality can't you live without?** What does everyone love? These questions can help you understand what content types and CMS features authors need.

Once the survey results are in, look for trends and extremes. Trends are places where everyone agrees. If 90% of your respondents marked adding an image as very time consuming, this is a place you can explore. What about this process is taking so long? What can be done to improve it? The lack of a trend can be informative too. If you get an even distribution of responses to how difficult a task is, why is that? Are there different types of functionality based on role or department? Are some authors getting better training or support than others? The same goes for the open-ended questions. What topics or tasks are people mentioning more than others? Are there any common themes across the answers?

Extremes can also be interesting. 90% of people identifying a task as very easy is great, but what if the other 10% rate it as difficult or very difficult? What is going wrong there? It might be worthwhile to identify these people and reach out to them to get a better understanding of why they are struggling while others are succeeding.

Interviews

One of the best ways to figure out who your authors are and what they're struggling with is to go right to the source. Sit down and talk to them. Interviews allow you to explore people's daily frustrations, identify functionality that is needed or missing, and establish big picture goals or priority issues to be fixed. If you hear multiple people talking about problems with document management or inconsistent design tools, then you know that this is something you need to figure out for the next iteration.

Interview protocol

Before you start interviewing, develop an *interview protocol.* This is a template that outlines everything an interviewer needs to conduct an interview: questions to ask, background information about the interviewees, introductory material, and any instructions for the people giving the interviews.

Keep the questions standard so you can cover the same topics with everyone and identify trends.

If you've already sent out a survey, you'll have some great starting data to inform your interviews. Confirm any inconsistencies from the survey, or places where you want to dig deeper, but don't spend too much time covering the same ground. If you haven't sent a survey, you can start fresh with some of the same basic questions.

Try these common interview questions about content (but skip over anything already covered):

- What is your title and primary job function?
- What portion of your job involves dealing with the CMS? (Entering content is often a small part of people's main job.)
- What kind of content do you enter?
- Who are the primary audiences for your site?
- How do you create content? How do you enter content into the CMS? Describe all the steps.
- What is the process for editing existing content? How do you find content, to edit it?
- What is and isn't working for you on a day-to-day basis?
- How do you hope this project will change your work?
- How would you measure success?
- What challenges are there to achieve those measures?
- Is there any existing documentation or documents I should reference, to learn more about the work you do?
- Is there anyone else I should talk to?

Many authors will focus on the system and its interface when faced with these questions. Encourage them to also talk about organizational or process issues that get in the way of them doing their best work. The biggest issues at an organization may have nothing to do with technology but are instead issues of process or organizational dysfunction. This is important to figure out. You can't solve organizational problems with a new CMS, but you can acknowledge them and try to figure out ways to build a system that works for the current reality.

Conducting the interview

Once your protocol is ready, go talk to some people! This is one of my favorite parts of a client project. Meeting people and hearing about the way they work is endlessly fascinating. Attend to it with a sense of curiosity and an open mind.

When choosing who to interview, aim to get a broad range of viewpoints that represent a cross-section of the organization's authoring community. You'll want people who are full-time web pros, but also dabblers who edit here and there. The biggest cheerleaders, and the crankiest curmudgeons. The largest departments, and the ones with five employees who are constantly forgotten. If your system needs to work for all these people, then you'll need to understand them. Surveys can help you identify people who meet your criteria.

Keeping to a standard set of questions will help you identify trends between interviews and provide structure you can fall back on when you finish discussing a specific topic. At the same time, you can veer in a different direction if you hear something particularly interesting during an interview session. When you hear a broad or vague statement like, "We need more design freedom," don't take it at face value. Dig into the reasoning behind it. What kind of freedom? Why do you need it? What goal or result would more freedom be in service of? Chasing down the specific answers to these unclear comments can help you zero in on what problems need fixing and on finding the right solutions.

Probe further when an author offers a solution to an unstated problem. A common example is something like, "I need a color picker to be able to make text multiple colors." What is the need behind this request? It might be, "I need better ways to highlight a passage of text," or it might be, "Our school colors are green and gold." These are different problems which require different solutions, but it's unlikely a color picker for text is the answer. Often you will find that what authors ask for is related to a much broader problem, and the solution is something completely different from what they think they need.

Another thing to listen for is the language and terminology authors use. Do they refer to a piece of functionality using words you wouldn't normally use? Do they use terms you aren't familiar with or are domain specific? Take note of this language as you're going through your interviews. It will help you communicate with authors by using phrases that are familiar to them.

Finally, ask your interviewee to show you their problem, if you want to get a clearer picture of it. I was recently at an interview in which an author complained that it took too many clicks to add a new piece of content. I was confused by this, as I knew it only took one or two clicks, so I asked him to show me. He pulled out his laptop and ran through his process. It turned out it was only two clicks, but he had to navigate a poorly designed nested menu to get to where he needed to go, and the labels he had to follow were not clear or intuitive. It *seemed* like more than two clicks due to cognitive overload. I never would have gotten this insight if I hadn't bothered to ask. Seeing people walk through a process, step by step, can create more clarity than a verbal explanation.

There is one final benefit of doing interviews with authors. Conversation builds connection and helps you identify cheerleaders for the project.

A colleague and I recently interviewed a woman who worked for a government agency. She had built their first website in 1997 and had been leading their web presence ever since. She was *very* protective of it, and not particularly thrilled with the idea of migrating to a new platform. (She said she would quit if she was forced into it.)

When we came in to interview her, she asked us about our priorities and what we thought the most important parts of the new system would be. It was like she was interviewing us and not the other way around. We talked about things like focusing on user needs, accessibility, and writing in plain language. The more we talked the more her eyes lit up. She loved all of those things and had been advocating for them for a very long time. We ended up spending most of the interview talking less about her system and more about how to improve information publishing in government and our approach to it. By the end of the interview, we had an ally, and by the end of the day she had gone to her boss to discuss what it might look like to migrate to this new platform.

This kind of connection only happens when you talk to people. So meet authors where they are, let them know they're valuable enough to listen to, and get them invested. There's no substitute for that kind of direct interaction.

Interviews are a great tool for gaining insights from individual authors, but they can only go so far. Sometimes you want the same personal touch that happens from direct interaction, but combined with an ability to spot trends and priorities. That's when you want to conduct workshops.

Workshops

Workshops are interactive activities where participants brainstorm and work through problems together. Like interviews, workshops help you get feedback directly from your users, but in a group setting instead of one on one. This allows for a different kind of feedback that takes advantage of group dynamics and consensus building.

Workshops also provide an opportunity to mix content authors with project stakeholders to see where priorities and goals are aligned or in conflict. If different user groups have different ideas of what's important, it's best to figure that out at the beginning of a project rather than in the thick of development.

One workshop you might run at the beginning of a project is an implementation of the K-J method (***https://articles.uie.com/kj_technique/***). This exercise collects the pain points and issues that users want to see addressed and prioritizes them. I colloquially refer to it as the "airing of grievances" exercise and it runs for about an hour. Here's how it goes:

- Give every attendee five sticky notes and three dot stickers. The dot stickers could be colored, based on their role (content authors, business stakeholders, developers, project managers, etc.) but this is optional.
- Ask attendees to write down the five biggest issues they have with their current website on the sticky notes. These can be about the design, functionality, authoring, or whatever drives them crazy. If they don't have five, that's fine, but five is the max. Give them five minutes to write down their concerns.
- One by one, invite each person to state their issue and describe how it affects them. You don't have to give a time limit, but you do want to keep things moving, especially if you have a lot of participants. As they read off each note, take it from them and put it up on a board. There should be no interruptions and no discussion. This is their time to talk. Some notes will be duplicates. Place those on top of each other so that you can tell how many are stacked.
- Start thinking about emerging themes. Are the complaints mostly about user experience or authoring? Are they about performance or design? What connections are you able to make between them as they come to the board?

- Once you're done, take a moment to condense the duplicates into a single note. Add a number to the top note so you can tell how many people brought up that subject. If several topics are similar, but not quite the same, group them together and give them a thematic title. For instance, there may be several different issues around how files are uploaded and used on the site, which you could condense into "document management."
- Once you've finished removing duplicates, condensing, and identifying themes, ask each participant to place their three dots on the items they believe are most important. (Yes! They only get to choose three!) Then rank the items based on the number of votes. What you end up with is a list of issues that are priorities for participants, ranked as they themselves voted for them.

Sometimes this ranked list comes with obvious things to address. That's great! Everyone agrees! More often, you will find some agreement combined with some conflict. Many organizations will already be aware of this tension. Some will be surprised, especially if this is the first time a cross-functional team has been brought into the room together. This realization can be a moment of clarity for a team, and the workshop is an opening to start talking about it. Getting the team to make a plan might be difficult, but you can't solve a problem you don't know you have.

It's possible to run a workshop like this online using tools like Miro or FigJam. However, online workshops are much more difficult and require more preparation. Many participants will not be familiar with the tools—you may need to have an extra facilitator dedicated to tech support. A couple of practice runs with a broad range of participants will help you get an idea of what kind of issues people encounter, so you can solve for them beforehand.

Whether online or in person, workshops and group exercises work best if you can create a base level of psychological safety. This allows people to feel like they can share freely, without fear of backlash or ridicule. There is often a power disconnect in these groups, with participants at the executive level mingling with people who are entering content on the website only part time. This can make people hold back concerns they want to address. You will not get what you need out of that atmosphere. Encourage everyone to bring their best, and treat all ideas as equally valuable, regardless of who they come from. If possible, try and hold space for everyone to say their piece. Allow everyone to read their notes without interruption or comment, and hold back discussion until the grouping is completed. This way, the more forceful voices can't drown out the people who might feel more hesitant about speaking up. Holding these lines can be difficult, but getting everyone's input is crucial if this process is going to be successful.

The great thing about workshops is that their interactive nature gets people engaged and interested. This isn't exactly news for the UX community, but for many content authors, this will be the first time they've been invited to participate in creating the product they use. Make the most of this opportunity. Lift them up and give them a voice. Their input is extremely important, and it's often at odds with priorities from other areas of the business. Opposing priorities can be hard to smooth out, but doing so is essential to building a system that works.

Scratching the surface

Research is vital for understanding your authors, their use cases, and how they fit into the greater project. If you don't understand your users, you can't build for them. And if you don't build for them, your system will be less successful than it could be. Research has the added benefit of getting authors to feel invested in the system. It gives them a sense of ownership, which has a long-term impact on your system's success.

Many people reading this book will be familiar with the standard UX research methods. This chapter scratches the surface of how those methodologies can be used to discover the needs of content authors. If you want to dive further into these topics, see the Resources section at the end of this book.

Now what do we do with all this research? How do we use it to create a better CMS for authors? Time to start prototyping?

5. Prototyping

If you're at all familiar with user interface design, then you're familiar with some type of prototyping. *Prototyping* involves taking a representation of the interface and putting it in front of users to see how they interact with it.

Prototyping is powerful because it is low effort but high value. Prototypes are often high-fidelity representations of an interface or user flow—but they don't have to be. A prototype can be as simple as a whiteboard and a bunch of markers and sticky notes. That simple workflow can yield valuable information.

Compare this to holding off on testing until you have built a functional CMS. Reworking months of development comes at a high cost. By that point it's too late—there is little appetite to tear things apart and start over again. Problems can be surfaced earlier with conceptual testing.

Setting the stage

Before testing any prototypes with content authors, make sure they understand the context of the work you're doing by telling them the following:

- Why are they here?
- What is expected of them?
- What are we hoping to learn from them?
- How can they give feedback?
- How will their feedback be used?
- How can they follow up later, if needed?

This level-setting effort will get them in the proper frame of mind for the work to come. This is especially true when working with authors who are not web professionals. They may not be familiar with the process of designing websites or user interfaces and the tools that are used for these projects. The more context and framing you can provide to these users, the more comfortable they will be and the more helpful the prototyping sessions.

There are lots of ways to prototype authoring tools, and lots of contexts in which to use them. Each has its pros and cons, depending on what you're looking to do and what information you're trying to get. We're going to talk about a handful here, just as a starting point.

Paper prototyping

The most basic type of prototyping is with paper. In this context, paper is "any writeable surface." At its most simple, *paper prototyping* can be done on the proverbial napkin, but the most common writing surface is some variety of whiteboard. What's valuable about whiteboards is their ubiquity in office spaces, so you don't have to worry about bringing or finding special tools. That said, when I go to client on-site meetings, I sometimes bring laminated pieces of 11x17 paper, which act as instant portable whiteboards. They are easy to carry rolled up, and you can lay them out on a table where people are gathered, which can help with interactive exercises. There are also a variety of whiteboard notebooks with multiple spiral-bound pages. I really like the NuBoard from Obun (***https://en.obun.jp/stationery/nu-board/***) but there are lots of other options.

Whiteboards may be ubiquitous, but there are great things about paper:

- **It's flexible.** Draw an interface to try out on users, and as they respond, wipe it away, or start over with a fresh sheet and make modifications. Once you're done, you have a perfect document you can take back to your office.
- **Everyone knows how to use it.** You don't have to set up any special technology or do tech support or have a specific browser version installed. You just pull it out and go.
- **It's cheap.** Th is is true not just in raw dollars but also in terms of the time expended to produce the prototypes. Test out major concepts with scrappy drawings and see how they land. Since they're so cheap to produce, failure is inexpensive, which gives you the opportunity to try out lots of different things with lots of different users.
- **It's fun.** Paper is tactile and gets users involved in a different way than poking at a screen does. When people interact with their hands rather than a pointer, you get different insights. Research (*https://pubmed.ncbi.nlm.nih.gov/28536546/*) has shown that writing triggers different parts of the brain and forces people to process ideas as they write, rather than push out unfiltered thoughts in real-time on a keyboard.

Prototyping content entry

I like to build up an entire set of screens on paper with a small group of content authors, and modify them along the way as different issues arise. This is helpful when you have a semi-complicated piece of content that integrates with different aspects of the system, like media or related content.

- Start with a *copy deck* for a piece of content they need to create, broken down into the different fields that need to be entered (more on copy decks in Chapter 9: Support).

- Draw a box on the whiteboard. This represents the title field.
- Then move to the next field. Maybe it's a hero photo (the giant, gorgeous photo that sits at the top of an article to attract attention and inspire people to read). Talk with content authors about where media entry comes in their process. Do they usually have the image when they begin working with this content, or do the words come first and is the photo added later? Is it disruptive to their process to enter text, then deal with media, then go back to entering text? Does it make more sense to deal with all their media in one place, rather than here and there throughout the interface?

As you dig into these ideas, start mocking them up on the whiteboard. Let's say your authors don't always have all the elements of their content when they start to create it. Maybe it makes sense to group the fields related to content they *do* have up front at the top, and then move the ones that come later farther down the page. So you try that, and they might say, "This is good, except we often have to change the hero four or five times because everyone is so indecisive, and in our current system, the hero is at the bottom of the page, and it drives me crazy to have to scroll all the way down there every time it happens." Ahhhh, now we're getting somewhere! Wipe it away and move the hero up towards the title. Repeat this as you move through the rest of the content elements.

There are many benefits to this activity, some obvious and some less so. Changing an interface by wiping away a white board is much cheaper than filing tickets to do it in the CMS. So you're already winning. You're also continuing to build bonds with content authors while getting them invested in the process. They get to see their feedback come to life. This can be incredibly validating and can go a long way to restoring a sense of trust in organizations where there has long been a lack of it.

As you continue prototyping, consider situations where context might impact the content process. For instance, is there a difference between how authors work when they create new content versus when they edit already published content? If one piece of content is reliant on some other content in the system, what is the process for getting the related content created if it doesn't already exist?

Prototyping page building

You can use prototyping to explore other kinds of interfaces as well. As we discussed in Chapter 2: Structure vs. Flexibility, many modern systems allow authors to build page layouts using reusable content blocks or components. This is a fundamentally different interaction than filling out fields for an article or event. Protoyping page-building interfaces ensures authors will be able to build the kinds of pages they need with the tools you create.

In this exercise, we use the 11x17 laminated sheets mentioned earlier, with a rough drawing of the site's header and footer already in place. Then we create index cards with wireframe representations of the different components that would be available to build those landing pages, such as a link collection, a list of teasers, and a call to action (**Fig 5.1**). We bring these laminated sheets and wireframe cards to site authors and ask them about the kind of content they want on their home page. As they talk, we start placing cards on the page to show how it might look. In time, the users will usually start to add, remove, or move the cards around the page themselves. In this way, authors will show you how they need to build their pages and what kinds of content they need to represent. Index cards are cheap, and if one isn't working, you can just throw it out and make a new one. If you need a new component you hadn't planned on, just write up a new card on the fly.

Fig 5.1: *Laying out index cards on erasable prototypes can help content authors visualize abstract content ideas in a way that increases understanding and invests them in the system being built. Drawing all those cards is pretty fun, too.*

You don't have to test an entire page, either. If you are debating variations on a specific component or interface widget, draw them out and show them to the authors. This can be done at any level of granularity. You could even meld this idea with the editorial user interface exercise at the beginning of this chapter (see Paper prototyping).

Prototyping exercises are much harder to conduct if you're not in the room with your users. Online prototyping sessions are a little easier if you don't allow workshop participants to modify the prototype. Leave this to facilitators instead. It's best if you have two facilitators—one leading the conversation and one making changes to the interface. This makes the workshop somewhat less engaging for participants but avoids the technical pitfalls involved when people try to work in whatever software you are using.

Paper prototyping is most useful early in a project, when multiple options are under consideration and you don't want to invest in any of them until you know they have a chance of working. Once you get a solid understanding of how you might put workflows together, you can start mocking up high-fidelity concepts to show to users.

Digital prototyping

As you move farther along in the CMS development process, it will make sense to go from paper to digital mockups of real interfaces. A *digital prototype* can also be done at any level of fidelity, but as we've discussed, the deeper into a project we go, the more costly changes will be. So the same principle applies here as it did for paper prototyping: the bigger the change, the earlier you should test it, with the lowest possible level of fidelity.

When people think of digital prototyping, they usually imagine wireframes. But we can get a lot of the same information from paper prototypes as we can from wireframes—and paper is cheaper and easier to work with. When moving into the digital realm, mock up screens with real form elements, and possibly some basic design, in an image editing tool. As you increase fidelity, you'll have opportunities for different kinds of testing.

For instance, once you have an interface designed to the level of fields, you'll be able to experiment with click testing.

Click testing

At its most basic level, click testing asks the user, "Where would you click to do <task>?" For example, you might give content authors some sample content, show them the screen where they create new content, and ask what content type they would choose to enter their sample into the CMS. Or, you could mockup a content entry screen and ask, "What field would you use to have this content publish automatically at nine o'clock tomorrow morning?"

Click testing can help you understand if:

- Authors know how to accomplish common tasks.
- Proposed interface elements make sense in context.
- Navigation, form, label, and help text language are clear and useful.

Click tests can be collected into a set and sent to authors to take on their own, without moderation. Have the authors identify themselves before they take the test so you can follow up with further investigation. There are many different tools that facilitate click testing (see Resources for suggestions).

After the test is complete, you should get some data about how many people successfully completed the test, often accompanied by a heatmap showing where everyone clicked. You'll also have some quantitative data about the percentage of users who completed the test successfully. Often the failures are the most intriguing. Why did 15% of users click this instead of that? Is it because the wording is ambiguous? Is the content placed on the screen in a location that has some other context? Success is great—but failure is where the real lessons are.

Failure is a win

Once you've identified areas of failure, the next questions should be, "Why did they fail?" and "How can we fix it?" If your authors identified themselves during testing, you can ask them about their thought process and choices.

On a project for a government client, we created a content type called Update, which was meant for things like news and press releases. When we tested this with users, they often failed to correctly identify when they should use this content type. Why? They were confused. They thought of "update" as a verb (like the equivalent of edit) rather than as a noun (you create an update). We changed the name of the content type to News, which was much more successful.

Have follow-up conversations without judgement. Lead with curiosity and openness. Leave words like "test failure" out of the conversation. The authors didn't do anything wrong, but you do need to understand their thought process to be able fix the issues they encountered.

Once you have the why, you can start coming up with the how—the solutions. Repeat tests to further refine potential fixes. Combine the click-testing with A/B testing when you're waffling between two options. Half the users get one option and half get the other. Which one is more successful? If you get a 50/50 split, is it because both are fine or because both are flawed?

Functional prototyping

A *functional prototype* is a working model of a product or interface. Creating functional prototypes can be simpler than you think. Many modern CMS platforms allow you to quickly build out some level of functionality using only the administrative user interface. This means that your CMS can become a place to mock up functionality and test it with users. All you need to do is stand up a demo site, throw together a form, and test it. The site is completely throwaway, and you can take what you learned into the implementation phase.

Those wireframes you built in the paper prototyping phase? Now you can mock them up in a usable form and have someone enter real content into them. Don't sweat how they look too much. Think about higher level stuff:

- Does the field order make sense?
- Have you captured all the information you need to capture?
- Does that field really need to be required?

Watching people work through a content entry form will provide insights that you hadn't expected. You might be really focused on a certain piece of functionality, but as the author enters content, they could run into a problem you never would have anticipated. Have a plan going into your prototyping session, but be open to explore whatever unexpected discoveries come your way.

Building the perfect beast

Different prototyping tools have different benefits. Paper prototyping is low effort but can only go so far in testing real functionality. Mocking up forms to test requires more effort but comes closer to mimicking real-world experience. What works best will depend on how your authors plan to use the CMS and what kind of information you're trying to gather during a prototyping phase.

By now you might be asking yourself if we're ever going to *build* something. When do we get to see all this work come to life? The answer is: right now. In the next chapter we'll talk about the principles of creating good editorial interfaces. You'll learn how to apply your research to the system you're building.

6. **Designing Forms**

HTML forms are one of the oldest features of the web, and when it comes right down to it, web content management is mostly filling out forms.

If you think that forms are straightforward and the standards around them are well known, in some ways you're right. There are lots of excellent resources for general form design (see Resources for suggestions). However, content entry screens have some differences. For example:

- Many forms on the web are meant to be filled out once and forgotten. In a CMS, a content author may revisit a form hundreds of times in the course of their work.
- Standalone web forms are usually designed to be short. CMS content entry forms can consist of dozens of interrelated fields that also tie together content from elsewhere in the CMS.
- General web forms are meant to work for anyone without any special training. For forms within a CMS, we offer training, documentation, and other resources to help users learn the system (more on Training in Chapter 9: Support).

Given how often an author will use the forms in a CMS, making them easy to use is vitally important. Our job is to make CMS forms feel approachable, to reduce clutter, and to help authors focus on the parts of the form that are most important. Together, these tasks reduce cognitive load. What is cognitive load, and how do we use this concept to make our forms more usable? Let's find out.

Cognitive load

Cognitive load theory, developed by John Sweller in the late 1980s, describes the mental effort needed to learn new things (*https://en.wikipedia.org/wiki/Cognitive_load*). Individuals can only hold so much information in their working memory. If working memory gets overloaded, learning becomes harder.

This concept can be applied to user experience design to describe the mental effort needed to learn and use a product. The greater the cognitive load, the more difficult a product will be to understand and use. This goes for content management systems, too. Content entry is complex, consisting of fields, taxonomy, metadata, and more. A well-designed authoring experience attempts to reduce that cognitive load.

Cognitive load is not a flat scale. The less familiar someone is with a concept, the more cognitive load it adds to their work. Your authors' backgrounds and the training you provide impacts their cognitive load. Content authors will also use your interface repeatedly, magnifying cognitive load.

Reducing cognitive load doesn't mean you should simplify your authoring experience so much that it undercuts the goals of making content in the first place. A CMS that is nothing but a title and a plain text body field is very simple, but woefully unprepared for modern content needs. The key is to build a system that is appropriate for your organization and authors, then to make it as easy to use as possible for their needs.

You can reduce cognitive load for your content authors by focusing on the design principles of proximity, consistency, and order. These are adapted from the Gestalt principles (*https://www.smashingmagazine.com/2014/03/design-principles-visual-perception-and-the-principles-of-gestalt/*), which define how people interpret what they see and hear.

Proximity

The principle of *proximity* states that people perceive objects close to each other as related, and objects farther away from each other as unrelated.

This concept is important in form design and can be used as the foundation for a usable authoring experience. Giving elements sufficient space makes it easier to identify individual elements and improves legibility. Content entry forms need to ensure that relevant fields are spatially related and that the words describing them can be easily read.

It might seem obvious, yet systems violate this principle all the time. Many systems cram form fields together to fit more fields on a single screen and to avoid scrolling—even though modern screen sizes vary so widely that optimizing towards what is or isn't on a user's screen is irrelevant. Pushing form elements together flouts the proximity principle by reducing authors' ability to tell which form elements are related (**Fig 6.1**).

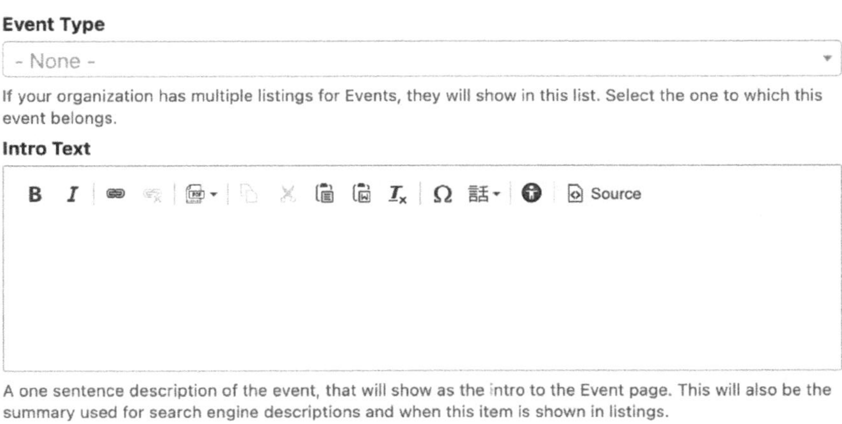

Fig 6.1: *Font weights help to distinguish these form elements from each other, but the limited spacing between them makes the overall form harder to scan.*

Best practice is to group related sets of form elements together and use other visual markers to indicate field relationships. For example, information for a location might require multiple fields for city, state, and postal code (**Fig 6.2**). All the form elements are grouped within a visual border, and the two street address fields are closer together than the rest, to indicate their relationship. The entire set of fields for event location can be collapsed using the caret at the top left of the set, so authors can minimize the fields when they are not in use, reducing the number of visible fields on the page.

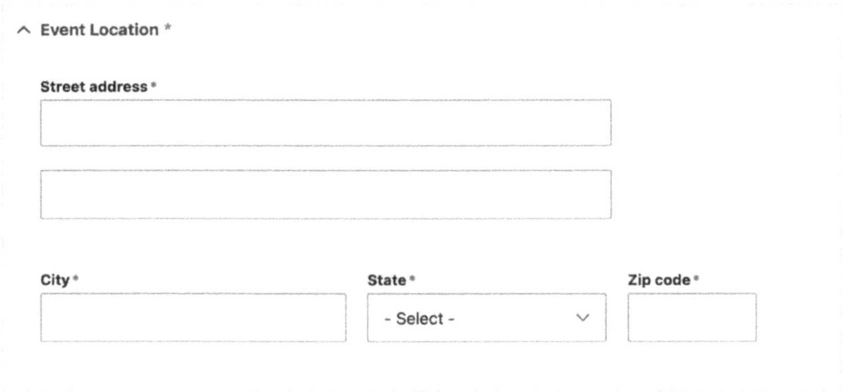

Fig 6.2: *This form takes advantage of proximity in two ways. All of the form elements are contained in a box with a label to indicate their relationship to each other. Within that box, the street address fields are closer together than the other fields, indicating that they also have their own relationship.*

Grouping is a powerful tool for reducing cognitive load, but it can go wrong if you don't implement it in a thoughtful way. You might be tempted to streamline a form by hiding groups of fields behind a tabbed interface (**Fig 6.3**) or in collapsed accordions. While those design choices reduce the amount of information presented up front, they also hide fields that authors are expected to use and obscure which fields are required. A new author might not figure it out immediately, resulting in entry errors that confuse them.

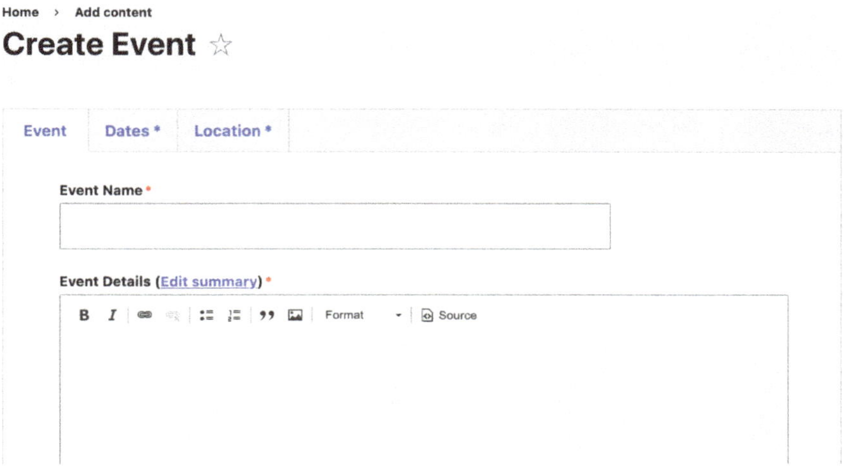

Fig 6.3: *This tabbed interface uses asterisks to indicate that each tab contains required fields, but the user has no idea how many fields are required or what their purpose is—assuming they notice the tabs at all.*

Clutter on a page is a symptom of other problems. If you have so many fields that you need to group them into tabs, your content model may be too complex and in need of restructuring. This is one of those places where good intentions (providing a large amount of flexibility to authors) can collide with reality (creating a content type that is so complex, it's difficult to use).

Clean, readable forms in the UI change a potentially frustrating experience into one that supports content authors and encourages them to use the system to its fullest.

Consistency

The *similarity principle* states that people create mental relationships between elements with shared properties, even if they are not near each other. Let's reframe the similarity principle as a focus on *consistency*. Similarity only works when elements are implemented consistently, allowing the meaning behind related elements to take shape throughout the CMS. Without consistency, there is no similarity. Here are some examples of how to bring consistency to content entry forms.

Use uniform naming conventions

Fields that do the same work should have the same name. For example, in many systems, content types have a short description field that is used as a summary in listings, and as the content's meta description. If you call this field "short description" in one place, "summary" in another, and "abstract" in a third, you are discarding information an author could carry from one place to another.

Place fields consistently

Consistency also applies to where a field is placed on the form. Something like the short description is probably best placed high up in the editorial interface, but it's more important that it goes in the same place on all the content types where it is used. Make sure authors never have to hunt for the right place to enter content.

This idea also extends to metadata and settings. Most content will have a setting to indicate if the page is published or unpublished. This field should be in the same place on every page. Not in the sidebar on some, and below the content hidden behind a tab on others. Identify settings and metadata that are the same across content types, and place them consistently.

Handle dynamic interfaces with caution

Some content contains fields that only apply in certain situations. For instance, an author could create an event that is online or in person. If the event is online, it needs a link to join the meeting. If it's in person, it needs a physical location address. A common solution to this is to show only the set of fields that applies to the choice the author made, preventing the author from having to think about irrelevant fields. This makes sense, but it can introduce problems:

- When authors edit existing content, the form will be different depending on their choices or the choices made by another editor.
- Authors may be confused if content in a field disappears. Was it saved? Where did it go?
- If the fields that change are offscreen, it's not obvious how an author's choices relate to the change.

Generally, an interface like this is fine if it adheres to the principle of proximity—the fields are close to where the choice is made, and the change to the form is clearly visible. Users expect that a form will be in the same state when they return to it after navigating away. If that isn't the case, consider whether a dynamic interface like this is worthwhile and test the interface to ensure that authors understand the way it works.

Use field widgets consistently

Field widgets specify how data is collected in a form. In a CMS, you can choose how to collect data in a field. For example, you could present a list of options using a drop-down list or radio buttons. If there are only two options, you could use a checkbox (or many checkboxes, if authors can select more than one item). Under the hood, these are all ways to enter a piece of text. The widget is the interface you use to collect that data (drop-down list, radio buttons, checkboxes, and so on).

These are important choices to make, so establish consistent standards for making them. You may need to ask your authors a yes or no question in multiple places in your system. There's no reason for one to be a checkbox, another to be radio buttons, and a third to be a drop-down menu. Consistency in widget selection will establish expectations for authors and reduce their cognitive load. Being consistent also scales understanding because authors can transfer the skills and knowledge they gain from one area of the system when they move into other ones.

Order

User-facing pages are designed with a content hierarchy in mind. The most important information goes at the top of the page, then the next important information, and so on, until you get to the bottom of the page (**Fig 6.4**).

A lot of thought goes into this hierarchy, so retain it for the editing interface as well. Set up your content types so that authors enter content in the same order as it appears on the page (**Fig 6.5**).

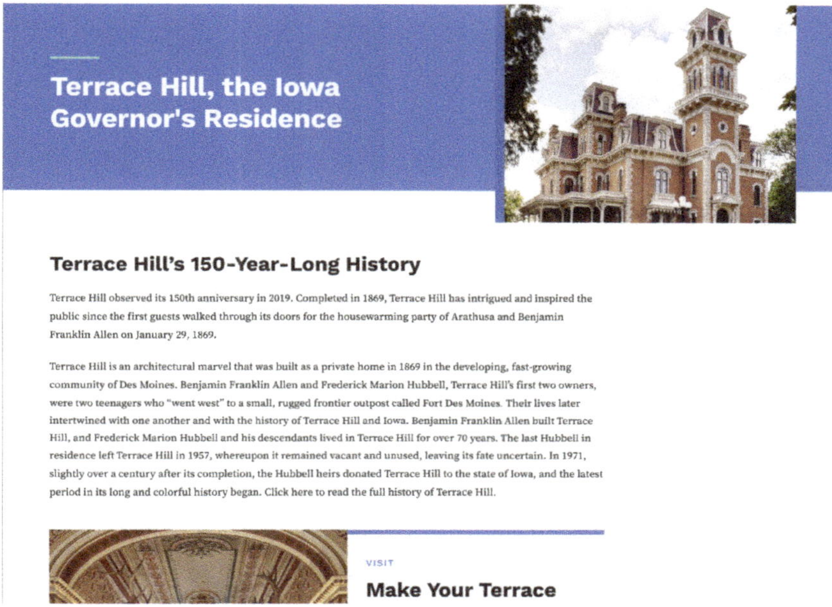

Fig 6.4: *The placement of content on this page indicates its hierarchy and importance. The title and image are of primary importance, followed by the subhead, body text, and call to action.*

When authors enter content into a system, they visualize how a page will look as much as they craft the words. This is especially true for subject matter experts and others who are not experienced content authors. Lay out content entry fields in the order authors expect, so they can focus on the content rather than trying to find the next field.

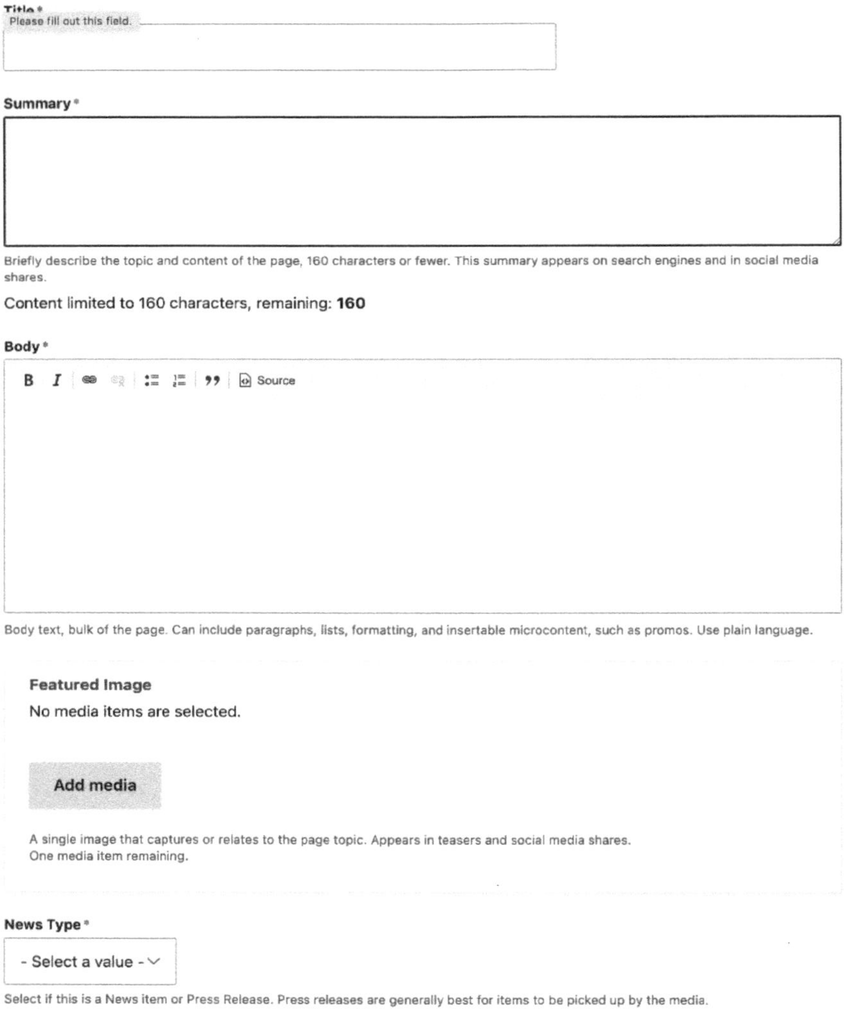

Fig 6.5: *Lay out content entry screens to reflect the content's hierarchy and how authors expect the content type's fields to be used.*

This is more of a guideline than a hard-and-fast rule. Content hierarchy should be the primary driver of how fields are ordered, but other factors can come into play:

- **Title**. The title should be the first field on the form. This is the content's identifier, both internally and externally, so having it first indicates its priority, even if it's not displayed first on the front end.
- **Metadata**. Some fields on the editing form, like metadata, are not displayed on the page. For example, earlier we discussed a summary field may be used in content listings or for social sharing but isn't otherwise shown to site visitors. We should place this field on the form near the title, which is its most closely related content. When the summary is shown, it's tied to the title, so it makes sense for these to have proximity. Use this same principle for other pieces of metadata.
- **Exceptions**. In this example, you would think the featured image field would be near the title if the image is displayed in the header. But that might not always be the case. For some organizations, having an image on posts might be rare, and even when that imagery exists, it might be low quality. In those cases, you could decide to de-prioritize the image field on the content entry screen, keeping it out of authors' way so they can concentrate on more important content.

Field ordering is something that is easy to dismiss or overlook, but it reduces cognitive load when it's done right.

Words as interface

> "The core of the interaction is the questions asked and answers given. This is why the words we use in the form, and not how it looks, are the most important part of the design.
>
> —Jessica Enders, Designing UX: Forms (*https://www.sitepoint.com/premium/books/designing-ux-forms/*)

Words are used in several contexts in authoring systems, each with their own purpose (Fig 6.6). As we've discussed, there are no one-size-fits-all rules for site authors. It's more important to know your audience and write interface copy for their needs. That said, there are some general guidelines which apply to almost any use case:

- **Keep it simple.** The mathematician Blaise Pascal famously said: "I have made this longer than usual because I have not had time to make it shorter." Take the time to make your copy shorter. Follow guidelines for plain language (see the Resources section for examples). The fewer words you use and the clearer they are, the easier your conversation with authors will be. Using concise language also improves the chances that someone with a cognitive disability will understand the text you write.
- **Use words your authors understand.** Keep the language of the CMS out of interface text and use the words your authors use. It's common for a CMS to have special terminology for pieces of content, like "nodes" or "leaves." These words have no meaning to most content authors. Replace terms like these with more common synonyms like pages or content.
- **Avoid directional language.** Directional language refers to an author's location relative to other elements on the page such as, "See the short description field below," or, "Use the sidebar options on the right." Page element placement is not always predictable and may change over time, on different devices, or when accessed with assistive technology. Your system will be more maintainable if this kind of language is avoided. Instead, refer to fields by their name or function.
- **Test it.** If you are concerned about your text's readability, test it with content authors. Your words are written for

real users whom you have researched and understand. Test it with those users to ensure they know what the interface is trying to say.

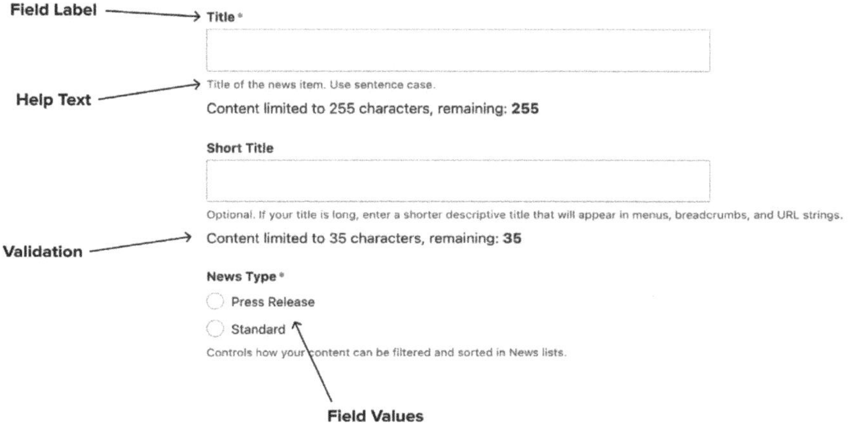

Fig 6.6: *Words are used to convey meaning in content authoring. The purpose of the text will change the kinds of words you choose to use.*

These are general writing guidelines for your authors, but specific elements have their own criteria. Let's look at some use cases in more detail, including labels, help text, and placeholder text.

Labels

Labels are used to name a field or user interface component, describing *what* it is. A label should be short and descriptive, so an author can immediately understand the purpose of the field. It should answer the question, "What is this?"

Different labels may be appropriate for interface items that have exactly the same functionality, depending on your audience or industry. Consider the following terminology:

- We have already talked about short description (or summary) fields. I use the label "short description" for this kind of field, because it's the most basic way to describe this element for a wide audience.
- In newspapers, the "dek" or "deck" is a short paragraph of text that runs immediately after the headline. Many sites in the journalism industry have carried this forward into their content management systems.
- In academic circles, the term "abstract" is used to provide a summary for academic papers and is often used for a summary field in academic CMS products.

None of these is wrong or right. They're all perfect for their own specific use cases. And that's the key to writing good labels: knowing your audience and having done the research to understand what they need and expect.

Many people in the content strategy and UX writing community have strong opinions about whether field labels should use title case ("Short Description Field") or sentence case ("Short description field"). Sentence case is generally easier to read, but for a formal label of this type, no research offers compelling evidence that it makes a difference. If your CMS provides a default, just use that. Otherwise make a choice and stick with it.

Finally, if you develop new fields or modify default CMS functionality, always enclose your field labels with the `<label>` tag, and properly associate your labels with their applicable form fields. This is a big win for accessibility, as screen readers will be able to read a form element's label when the element gains focus.

Help text

Help text helps authors understand *how* a field is used. If labels answer the question "What is this?" then help text should answer the questions "Why is this important?" and "How is this used on the website?" Help text should be short while still conveying information the author needs to get their job done.

Avoid help text that repeats the label name. For example, on a summary field, the help text "Enter a short description of this content" offers nothing beyond what the field label already does. Instead, try to add relevance:

> A summary of the content on this page. Used as the description in search engine previews, social media shares, and site listings.

This gives the author more context about how the field is used and where it will appear, both inside and outside the website.

Other jobs that help text can perform:

- **Describe validation requirements or special formatting.** Use help text to describe any requirements up front, such as character limits or phone number formatting. That way, authors will understand what is required before the form is submitted and they get a frustrating error message.
- **Highlight fields that affect the content's display.** Include help text when a field or option has a significant impact on the content's appearance or layout. Such changes should be described so that the author will understand the implications of choices they make. In some systems, you can write more extended help text (usually hidden behind a tool tip or icon) that allows for robust formatting or imagery. While you won't want to go overboard with this functionality, you might find it useful to show

authors what their changes will look like, rather than just telling them.

- **Explain parts of the system.** Help text is also used to describe different aspects of the system, such as content types or items in navigation. For system descriptions, the same concept applies. A label should describe the system part, and the description should explain why and how that part should be used.

Ensure your help text is fully accessible to those using assistive devices by using the `aria-describedby` attribute . This attribute tells a form element what other element contains the text that describes its use. When someone using assistive technology tabs into this element, the label and description will be read out to them.

As an alternative to help text, some CMS systems offer a way to add links to a URL as contextual help for a field or other UI elements. On the plus side, this allows you to maintain documentation in a single place outside the CMS, like a knowledge base. On the minus side, taking the user out of the context of the form they're filling out can be disorienting. It's also harder to do this in a way that is fully accessible, especially if you're linking to outside software. Sounds like a great place to do some testing with your users!

Finally, not every field needs help text. Many parts of the user interface are self-explanatory from their label. For instance, the label "Event start time" succinctly explains itself. Unless there are special requirements for this field, like validation, adding help text is redundant and adds cognitive load.

Placeholder text

Placeholder text is help text that is displayed inside a field. When an author starts to type into this field, the placeholder text disappears and is replaced by whatever the author types (**Fig 6.7**).

Fig 6.7: *Placeholder text within the field is often used to reduce the number of elements on a form.*

This may seem like a better option than help text underneath the field. It reduces clutter on the page, right? But in reality, it can cause several challenges:

- Once placeholder text disappears, the author loses valuable context about the field. Content entry forms are often long and detailed, and this context can be valuable as an author prepares content, often across multiple sessions. Permanent help text will always be there for reference.
- Placeholder text is usually displayed using a lighter color than help text and other labels on the form. This creates a low-contrast ratio that can be difficult to read. While this can be fixed using CSS, it can also make the placeholder text less distinct and readable from the label and help text.
- When placeholder text is used in lieu of field labels or help text, it causes problems with error handling. It becomes more difficult to refer to a specific field to check for errors because its "name" is gone once authors type in it.

In short, bypass inline placeholder text and use well-written labels and help text instead. If you do use placeholder text, make sure it complements labels and help text, not replaces them.

Validation

Validation is the automated process for checking that a field has the right value before an author submits it. Many CMS content fields have rules. They might be for formatting (product numbers are ###-#####-#########) or for length (minimum of 10 characters, maximum of 80), or certain information might be required. One way or another, you're going to need to make sure that the information authors enter is coming through the way you want or need it to. Here's how to make validation more author friendly.

Validation vs. coercion

In his book *Real World Content Modeling* (***https://deanebarker.net/books/real-world-content-modeling/***), Deane Barker explains the difference between validation and coercion. *Validation* requires checking input and displaying an error when content is incorrect. For example, if the author enters content that is not a number into a plain text field that requires a number, the system will show an error.

Coercion prevents incorrect data from being entered in the first place. If we want the author to only enter a number, we can use an HTML number field instead of a plain text field (**Fig 6.8**). This prevents authors from entering non-number values, and can also enforce minimum and maximum values. We make it impossible to make a mistake.

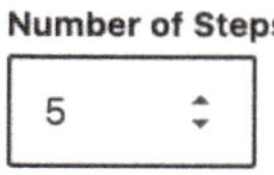

Fig 6.8: *The HTML number field type allows users to increase or decrease a number using up and down arrows on the right.*

Another example of coercion is setting a length on form elements, which prevents users from entering too much content into fields where there are limits (**Fig 6.9**). You can also use functionality like date pickers to encourage authors to not enter information by hand at all.

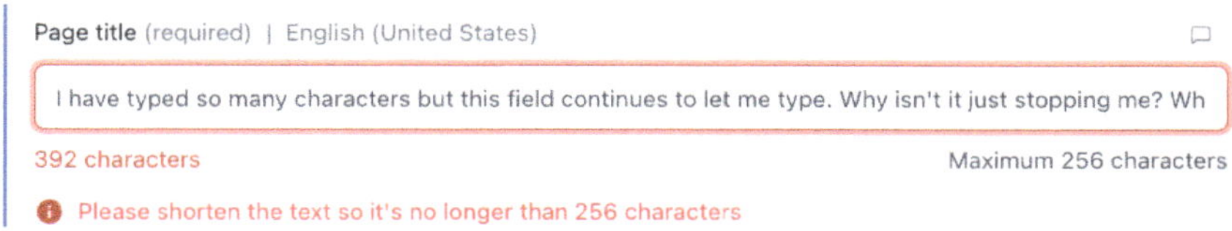

Fig 6.9: *This title field allows users to enter far more than the maximum 256 characters, forcing them to go back and fix the content when it can't be saved.*

Coercion is preferable to validation, because it provides clarity and prevents errors. Errors are one of the most disruptive aspects of entering information into a web form, so preventing those errors should be a high priority in your authoring interface.

Unfortunately, there will be times when coercion won't work, and you'll need to validate user input. One example is required fields. You can't prevent users from *not* entering something in into a field. You could potentially show a warning if they tab past a required field, but there are plenty of valid reasons why a user might do this, and repeated real-time warnings can be more disruptive than infrequent publish-time ones.

Use validation sparingly, and when errors happen, make them easy to identify and fix.

Handling errors

Sometimes things go wrong, and despite your best efforts, the system has to display an error to prevent the user from submitting invalid content. Errors are frustrating for users in the best of circumstances. They interrupt the flow of work and can be exasperating when an author is finally done with some piece of content they've been sweating over.

Worst of all, an error used to mean that work was not saved, and authors were in danger of losing their changes until the error was cleared. This is no longer true in many modern systems, but that trauma is ingrained in authors who have been doing content management for a long time. Reduce stress on your authors by managing errors thoughtfully.

What's true for labels, help text, and placeholder text is also true for error messages: they should be clear, readable, and meaningful. Error messages should also do the following:

- **Not blame the user.** Avoid "you" messages such as "You didn't enter a title" or "You need to enter a date in the format dd/mm/yyyy." Instead, use a message like "The title is required" or "Please enter a date in dd/mm/yyyy format." It may seem like a little thing, but putting these problems back on the user increases their frustration and reduces their confidence.
- **Help the author solve the problem.** "The date is invalid" is not useful if a user doesn't know what a valid date looks like. Instead, "The date must be in the future" explains what the problem is and how the author needs to fix it.

- **Appear all at once.** It is beyond frustrating to submit a form, get an error, fix it, resubmit the form, and get a different error. Show all errors when the form is submitted, and give authors the opportunity to fix them in one shot.
- **Be easy to spot.** Group all errors at the top of the page rather than distributing them throughout the form—they'll be easier to see and will offer authors an overview of what to fix before moving on. This is also ideal from an accessibility standpoint, as assistive devices can report all the errors at once. If your system already reports errors at the top, provide a jump link from each error to the field where it occurs, so users can easily get to where they need and make their fixes.
- **Use the `aria-invalid` attribute.** This allows assistive devices to inform users that a field has invalid data. If your errors are onscreen text notifications that don't rely solely on color, this isn't strictly necessary. But it's a helpful enhancement for people who are using assistive devices.

Unfortunately, in many systems, error handling is so baked into the code that modifying it to be usable and accessible is a real chore. Use these recommendations to guide functionality you build yourself, and—who knows—maybe some CMS developers and vendors will see these guidelines and use them to improve their systems for everyone.

Required fields

Required fields are a pain for authors when they're unnecessary and hard to spot. If authors don't notice a field is required, they won't fill it in—and they'll be frustrated when they get an error upon saving. It makes no sense to publish an event without a date, or an article without a title, yet required fields can get in the way of content authors and their workflow. They may be a necessary evil, but we can still make required fields less painful.

When a field must be required, do the following:

- **Label it clearly.** A common standard is to add an indicator (an asterisk) to field labels for required fields. Where you place the indicator relative to the label is not that important, as long as placement is consistent throughout the system. Required field indicators may use a different color, so they're highlighted. To support color blind users, color should never be the only indicator that a field is required.
- **Make it visible by default.** As discussed in the section on grouping, related fields are often collected in a tab group or behind a collapsible `fieldset` tag, such that they are not visible by default. It's confusing for site authors to receive an error on a required field they can't see in the first place. If you use these kinds of grouping interfaces, make required fields visible by default.
- **Add a default value.** Most systems allow you to specify a default value for a field. This allows the form to save necessary information without forcing the author to enter it, but still allows them to change it if they need to. The downside here is that if you specify a default, many authors will skip that field entirely, even in situations where they should change the value. You'll need to weigh those two scenarios to see which one works better for your situation.
- **Require only on publish.** Another consideration is whether the field needs to be required from the onset of content creation or only when ready to publish. Many CMS products allow fields to be blank while content is

being drafted but require the fields be filled in before the content is published. This allows authors more freedom to draft content in pieces before it goes live. For example, an author may have most of the information necessary to create an event, but they're still waiting on confirmation of the location. They need a location in order to go live, but they should still be able to save the information they already have and then come back to finish once they have all the details.

- **Help users find and fix errors.** If the system must present an error, it should be clear and visible. We've discussed this in detail in the section on error handling.

Custom interface components

Ideally, authors are already familiar with most of the interface elements in a CMS. Such elements are used widely on forms across the web, and authors probably encounter them repeatedly as they order products and respond to surveys. These common interface tools are great, because if authors and designers have been using them for some time, then they are already well vetted.

But what happens if you need some kind of custom interface component? Unless you have a very good reason, you're usually better off avoiding custom interface elements. The overhead required to develop, test, and iterate on custom elements is significant. So the best thing you can do when you're considering a custom element is to ask yourself, "Is this something that I really need to do? Will it bring significant value to the authors of my system?"

I had a client whose system allowed authors to add icons to pieces of content to help highlight certain subjects and provide graphic interest. In their old CMS, authors chose an icon by clicking a button and getting a file selection dialog for the central folder where those icons were stored. This caused a lot of problems with authors. The icons had no image previews, so authors had to know the filename to find what they wanted. Also, the filenames were not always intuitive, so the icons were hard to find, even when sorted alphabetically.

The team targeted this as an area we could improve. We designed a dropdown for the icons with human-readable names, and an inline icon preview (**Fig 6.10**). It also had type-ahead search that matched a word anywhere in the name, making the search much easier. This was not functionality provided natively by the CMS, so we had to develop it ourselves.

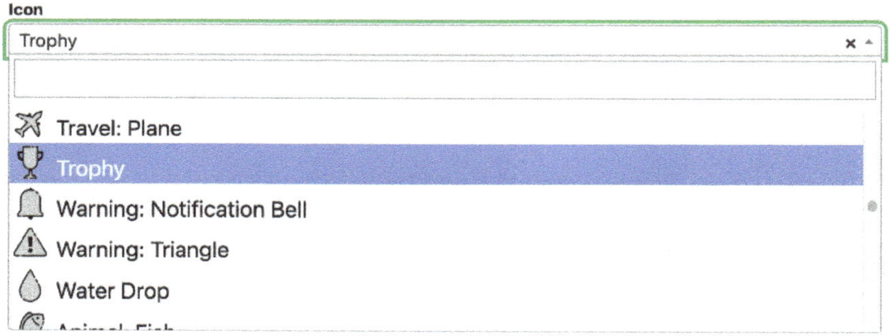

Fig 6.10: *Custom user interface elements can bring new functionality to life for content authors, but they can also cause new problems if they aren't tested properly.*

Many aspects of this widget might work functionally from a code perspective but fail from a user perspective. Here's what we needed to think about:

- **Will this work well on touch screens?** The click area for each icon seems small. Ensure that it's large enough for users to hit consistently.

- **Can users understand what this is?** The more options we show, the more they will understand that this is a list of icons with descriptions. Are we showing enough icons per page to get that message across, or do we need to make the page larger?
- **Can users find what they need?** Are the names well written enough that users can find the icon they want? Some of these icons have descriptions which apply to different ways of searching: "Warning" applies to a use case, and "Triangle" applies to the icon's shape. This is helpful for users who may have different needs.
- **Is this functionality accessible?** How will this work for people who are entering content using alternative interfaces such as screen readers? Anytime you create custom functionality you need to make sure the interface is fully accessible (more on this in Chapter 8: Accessibility).

These issues are hard to resolve without putting functionality in front of people and having them interact with it. Before creating new interfaces, ask yourself if you're really adding value over more well tested solutions. If so, make sure you do the necessary work to ensure your custom functionality is a success.

Half the battle

Content entry is the main use case for a CMS, and form design is the central functionality for content entry. The biggest thing you can do to prevent user frustration is to create well-designed forms that support the way your authors use the CMS. This applies not just to how the forms function, but also to the way you organize the information on them—and to the words you use to communicate with users. Give these forms the attention they deserve, and your authors will thank you.

Your work is not done, though. There are many other aspects of the CMS to be discussed. Content entry means authors can add and edit content, but they also need to be able to find content and know which tasks are a priority. Let's move from content entry to content administration.

7. Content Administration

In the last chapter, we discussed how you can help authors enter content by designing forms that reduce cognitive load. Now let's talk about the tools and workflows that will help your authors find and manage the content they create.

Content administration includes tasks such as:

- Choosing which content type to use.
- Finding, connecting, editing, publishing, and archiving content.
- Logging in and orienting to content tasks in the CMS.

That's what this chapter is all about. In organizations with large content operations, this might mean complex workflows or extensive editorial dashboards. But even if you have two part-time content authors creating one or two posts a week, you will find something useful in this chapter.

Editorial dashboards

The authoring experience starts immediately, right after the author logs into the CMS. What's the first thing they see? Often it's a list of recent content with search options. That's OK, but a personalized experience gets authors where they need to go faster. An easily accessible dashboard prevents authors from having to hunt for content or rely on systems outside the CMS to keep track of it. This reduces cognitive load and allows authors to focus on what's important to their work.

Dashboard elements

CMS dashboards are not all the same. They can contain multiple elements or blocks, with lists or other information within them. Which elements are appropriate for your dashboard will depend on your organization and author roles. Again, designing the best experience means knowing the needs of your organization and authors.

Here are common editorial dashboard elements:

- **Work in progress.** This refers to unpublished content the author is working on, or changes to published content the author is responsible for. This could be their own content in progress, other authors' content they need to review, content ready for publication, or any combination of these. What's important is that authors are able to find content that specifically requires some kind of action from them. Have this kind of task list in a central and easily accessible location, to help authors track their content in the same tool they use to create and edit it. You'll increase efficiency and improve the author's focus.
- **Alerts.** Many CMS systems integrate with tools like Siteimprove (*https://siteimprove.com*) or Monsido (*https://monsido.com*) , which track content issues like accessibility problems, broken links, and poor readability. Add this data to the dashboard, prioritized by what your organization values, to alert authors to issues that need their attention. Limit alerts to flag content that a signed-in author is responsible for, since that's the content they can fix.
- **Functional tasks.** This is a list of links to tasks that authors perform often and can include things like creating content, managing uploaded images and

documents, and searching for content. Tasks that are common for one role are not necessarily common for another, so the dashboard should reflect that or allow authors to customize their own list.

- **Documentation and support content.** This includes links to documents that help authors answer questions or that support their content creation process. Common examples include style guides, training materials, and upcoming events such as office hours or lunch-and-learn sessions.
- **News.** Includes announcements of updates to the system, new functionality, and upcoming maintenance windows.

Use these as ideas as inspiration. Every system will have different needs and priorities. The most important thing is to understand your authors and how they work, so that you can provide them with the most needed and useful dashboard information. Without that background, you're just guessing.

Dashboard personalization

An editorial dashboard should be personalized to a signed-in user's needs. A previous example mentions limiting content lists to what the current user is working on, but you can extend personalization into other areas. For instance, if you display tools to run a set of reports or processes, don't display them to users who don't have permission to access those tools. You might even want to customize parts of the dashboard for different roles, focusing on the most common tasks and priorities for each.

Other contexts can come into play as well:

- What are the needs of a user who is new, versus one who has been using the system for five years?

- Are there tasks that are common during one time of the year but not another ?

Identify these use cases in your research phase, and start putting them to work.

I once worked on a CMS built for an organization supporting independent booksellers that allowed bookstore owners to run their own websites. Their dashboard offers extra functionality to help booksellers manage orders and integrate with payment processors (**Fig 7.1**). Selling books is a high priority for their business, so the top of the dashboard focuses on those activities, providing a clear update of how many orders are in what states and linking to order management tools.

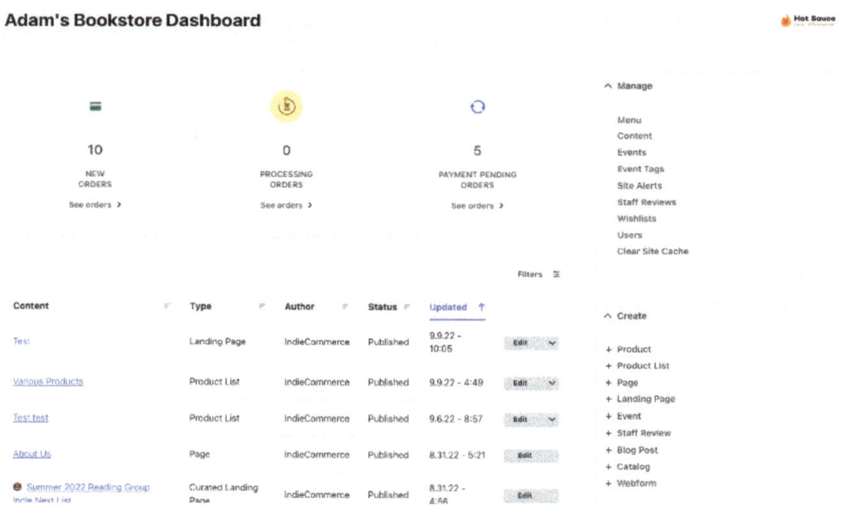

Fig 7.1: *This dashboard for a CMS focused on selling books highlights statistics on the store's performance, as well as recently published content and quick links to common tasks.*

"Content" can mean different things in different contexts and systems. Not all tasks that authors carry out in their CMS have to do with content as we usually define it. Allow quick access to valuable tasks, whether they have to do with website content or something else entirely.

Understanding content types

Creating new content is a common author task, and the first step in content creation is to choose a content type. Content types define the fields and metadata that a piece of content needs in order to serve a business purpose. The needs of an event are different than the needs of a blog post or those of a product page. Content types turn business and user needs into fields in a form. Authors enter information that's appropriate for the content and ensure it will be displayed in the right context on the site.

Unfortunately, content authors often choose the wrong content type for their content, especially in organizations with weak governance. This might be because one content type is more flexible and they prefer it to another content type that is more restrictive, or because they don't understand how or why content types differ. When you guide users to choose the proper content types for their content, the result is better performing content and a better user experience for site visitors.

Differentiating content types

Sometimes, the choice of content type is straightforward. Nobody is going to choose to create an event when they need to create a blog post. (Although I've encountered plenty of situations where authors will do the reverse.)

Other times, the distinction between content types is less clear. Imagine two content types, one called News and the other Press Release. When an author goes to select one of these content types, they might see choices like these:

News: Update, announcement, or other timely post.

Press Release: Official statements to provide to the media.

These descriptions don't sufficiently explain the difference between these two content types. They say *what* they are, but not *why* an author might choose one or the other. Think back to the research you did. What are the author use cases? What do they encounter in their day-to-day work? How can you use that information to help them understand what a content type is for?

One short description doesn't give you much room for this context. What if we added even more information? One example (**Fig 7.2**) adds several pieces of information designed to help authors make better decisions.

- **Description of use.** In the example below, authors learn where news posts will be located on the site and that this content type isn't appropriate for official updates. For the press release, authors learn that they can't use images. This is a good cue—the description helps authors know to choose a different content type if they need to use images.
- **Page thumbnails and icons.** Authors don't often think of their content's use or function. Instead, they imagine how it will look after it's created. Include a thumbnail of the page design to give them something to visualize. When an author sees that the news content has photos, but the press release content doesn't, it clues them in to which is better for their planned content—even if they don't bother reading the descriptions. Icons provide another way to visually differentiate between content types.
- **Links to other content of this type.** These links allow authors to see examples of how this content type is used. Authors can learn from what other people have done.

This can be especially valuable for new users who are still learning what's available and how content is built.

With this extra context, authors will have better information and be able to make decisions that are in line with the needs of the content and their organization.

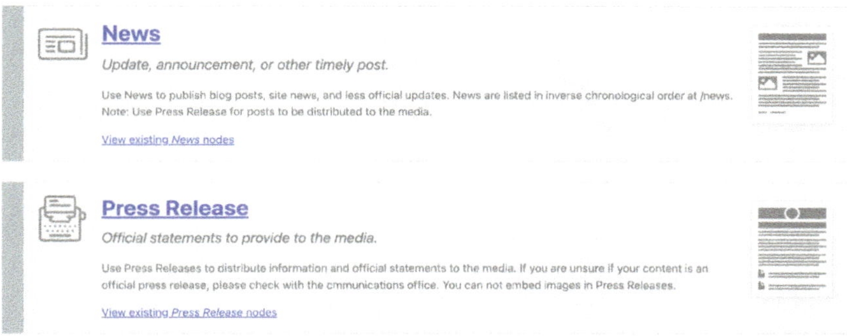

Fig 7.2: *Providing extra context, such as a longer description and imagery, can clarify use cases for content authors and lead to better decisions.*

Display customization

The needs of new users are different than the needs of seasoned users. When we tested this interface with a client's authors, they complained that the extended descriptions and imagery took up a lot of screen real estate, requiring them to scroll to get to the content types at the bottom. Experienced system users have a better handle on what the content types are and when to use them, so this extra information is not helpful. We added a toggle to put the listing into a grid view, which optimized screen real estate (**Fig 7.3**). Now, once an author gets used to the system, they can choose grid view to get to what they need quickly.

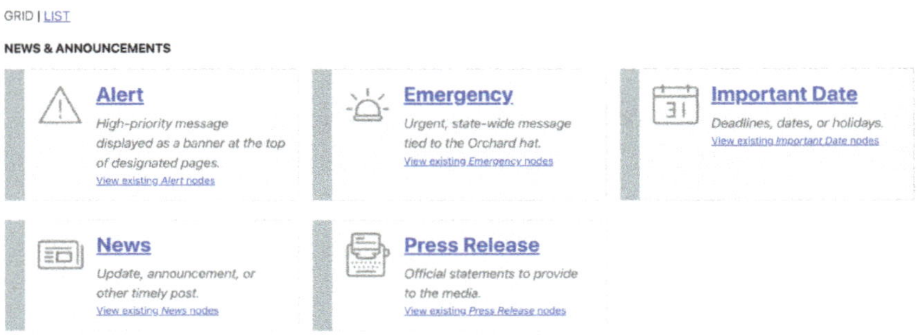

Fig 7.3: *Different views of the same information can help users in differing contexts, depending on their experience or role.*

Another feature we implemented was the ability to mark a content type as a favorite, which moves it to the top of the list. Maybe an author works in public relations, and all they do in the CMS is create press releases. They shouldn't have to scroll to find the press releases every time.

This functionality was not cheap to build. It involved a lot of code and customization, but the client agreed it was a worthwhile investment. Content types are designed to fit specific circumstances. When authors choose the wrong content type, it can make a mess of your organization's website. Guiding authors to choose the right content type is an investment in content governance and in a sustainable CMS.

Content relationships

One major use case for any modern CMS is to reference or relate pieces of content. Think about an event with a location. In a very simple system, you enter all the details for the event and its location into the event body field. If there's another event at the same location? Just copy and paste the location information into the next event. This is a problem, because if any information about the location changes, it's very difficult to update. Someone has to find all of those events and edit them individually.

In a well-designed system, the event and the location are two independent pieces of content. When a content author creates the event, they select a location that already exists in the system, creating a relationship between the two. If the location phone number changes, it needs to be updated in one place only: on the location content element. That change is then reflected on all the events related to it. The result is less content duplication, less work, and a more maintainable system.

This important functionality adds complexity to the authoring experience. It's much easier to paste information into a text field than to deal with finding and relating pieces of content. So this functionality must be easy to use. There are two use cases I focus on to make it easy for authors to relate content:

- **Finding related content**: how authors find the content they want to relate.
- **Creating new related content**: what happens when authors need to create related content that doesn't exist.

Finding related content

To connect related content, authors need to be able to find the related content they need and select it. In a system with a couple of dozen options that authors are familiar with, a simple drop-down list will work. Systems with a larger volume of content, or authors who aren't sure what's in the list, will need a different solution. One option is to use a search field that allows the user to type in a title or phrase to find the appropriate content, which they can then select (**Fig 7.4**).

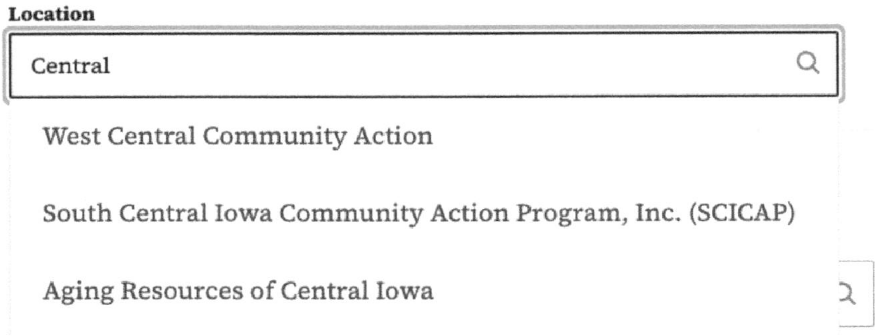

Fig 7.4: *This search interface allows authors to search for related content without having to scroll through a long list of options.*

These options work well for simple situations, but if your system has a lot of content with similar titles, things can fall apart quickly. In more complex cases, you might instead offer a modal or second screen with search and filter options (**Fig 7.5**). If your system has many locations, as in the example above, or if many of the locations have similar names, then adding a filter for address or ZIP code will help authors find the content more quickly.

These methods will help ensure authors find the content they need.

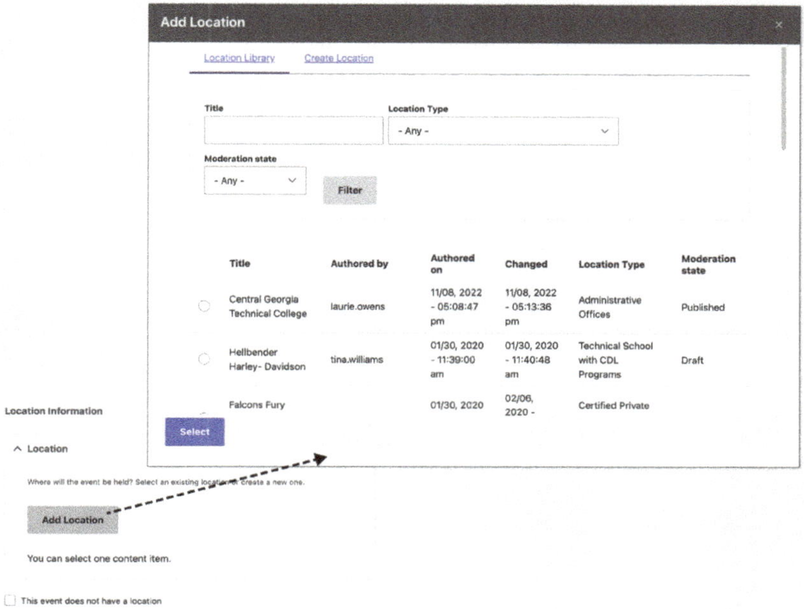

Fig 7.5: *In this interface, users can filter and sort a listing of locations, then select the one that matches.*

Creating new related content

Things change when the related content doesn't yet exist. For example, a content author is adding an event to the system, but when they get to the location field, they realize that the location they need hasn't yet been created. In many systems, the author would now have to leave the event they're working on to create the location. In the worst-case scenario, a filled-out location field is required to save the event, making it impossible to create the location and also save the work they've done so far. In these systems, authors have to create content in exactly the right order to avoid any problems—and that's not realistic. Let's give authors some better solutions.

- **Related content shouldn't be required to save work in progress.** If that content is necessary, such as an event's location, a better solution would be to make the field required to publish, not required to save. This lets authors save their work in progress while they go and sort out what needs to be done with their related content. (More about this in Chapter 6: Designing Forms.)
- **Creating new content shouldn't require abandoning the current context.** The most common implementation is a modal. Authors create the new content in the modal and return to the original content when it's done. In some systems, a new form opens dynamically right inside the main content. Either way, the user can create the related content as a part of their central authoring experience, without losing context and interrupting their work (**Fig 7.6**).

The concept of related content can be tough for a lot of content authors, requiring them to understand how pieces of content interrelate within a system. Tools that allow authors to relate content easily will help create a clean, maintainable content management system.

Content curation

When building out a website, there are many places where you will want to present lists of content. This could be an entire page, like a list of recent blog posts, or it could be more contextual, like a related content section at the bottom of an article. The one common property of all these lists is that the content needs to be *curated*. Somehow the system needs to know what content to list in which areas.

Curated content lists can be built manually by the content author or automatically by the system.

Fig 7.6: *In this system, an author can create a new author for their article by clicking the Create button next to the Author field. This brings them to a new screen, where they can ether the author's information. Once they publish, they retur to the original screen with this new author selected and all their work still intact.*

Manual curation

Let's say you have a marketing landing page with a list of featured case studies. The case studies in this list are important because the primary purpose of this page is to push people through the sales funnel. In this case, you might design the system so that the content author chooses which three case studies to include, tying them to current marketing priorities. When an author creates the content list, it's called *manual curation*. Manual curation is best when you want to:

- **Highlight specific content**, for specific reasons, such as on your homepage or major landing pages.
- **Allow re-ordering**, in case you need to move content from one spot to another.

Manually curated content involves relating pieces of content together, so the principles we laid out earlier on related content will serve you well.

Some organizations want to manually curate all of their content lists. They believe these lists are too important to entrust to the system. This instinct often backfires, however, especially for something like a Related Content list that appears on every blog post. Manually curated lists are a lot of work to maintain. If you remove a piece of content, and it has been manually linked to in several lists, then those links will now 404. Possibly worse is a linked article that goes out of date. You may have newer content that would be more appropriate in your lists, but making that change would require authors to find all the references and update them.

Content curation also increases cognitive load. Authors may not be clear about what list criteria are, what content is available to fill them, and how these choices impact user experience. That's where automated curation can help.

Automated curation

In some cases, manual lists don't make sense. Instead, the CMS can generate a list based on certain criteria, such as a list of all the published posts with a specified taxonomy term, ordered by date. This is *automated curation.*

Automated curation is best when you want to:

- **Offer related reading and content recirculation.** Lists that link to content similar to what the user is currently reading are good targets for automation. These lists usually appear on every piece of content in a type, for instance, a "Further Reading" list in the sidebar of every article that shows other articles on the same topic. With manual curation, an author has to choose two or three related pieces every time they create a new article. Automated curation saves time.

- **Update automatically.** Another big advantage of automated lists is that as time goes on, the lists can be updated without author intervention. If you have a list that shows the three most recent articles for a topic, and an author adds a new article that meets the list's criteria, then that list will be updated everywhere. The same goes for when content is deleted. Use a combination of recency and structured taxonomy to build lists that fulfill your purposes without adding to your content author's workload.

Be conscientious with your automated content curation systems. Poorly designed metadata can inadvertently create unfortunate content pairings—and offend users.

Finding content

Sometimes, content authors are not creating new content but editing existing content. There are two ways they ordinarily go about this task:

- They browse to a page and enter the editing interface directly, using a link provided to logged-in users with the appropriate permissions. If the author knows where a piece of content is on the site, they can find and edit it. This is straightforward, especially for authors who are familiar with a site and know where everything lives.
- They find the content in the CMS administrative interface. This is helpful if they don't know what the page is called or where it's located in the site structure.

In both these cases, authors can't edit content if they can't find it. Having difficulty with finding content in the system is a common problem and a red flag for larger issues in your CMS. If your content authors—who know your content well—can't find what they're looking for, how will site visitors be able to? Improving findability for your site authors can have a positive impact, system wide.

Every system comes with a default way to find content. These usually come in one of two flavors: list and search.

List

In this paradigm, authors see a list of all content and choose the item they want. Authors can winnow the list by searching (using text to find content in the title, body, or other fields) and filtering (finding content that matches a specific property, like whether it has been published or the date it was published). Filter options are usually predefined and represent what a typical user might want to see (**Fig 7.7**).

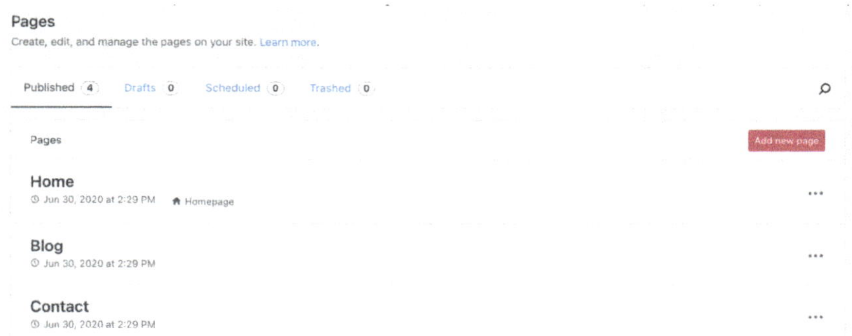

Fig 7.7: *In this system, a list of content can be limited by searching using the magnifying glass at the top right, or filtering to view content that is saved as a draft, scheduled to be published, or trashed.*

Search

In another common paradigm, authors see a blank search interface where they can enter terms and possibly choose filters. They'll see a content list only after searching or filtering. In a system like this, filter options are broader and are sometimes expanded to any number of fields in the system rather than presented as a pre-defined set (**Fig 7.8**).

This interface is very flexible, but more complicated. Authors might not know all the options available or how to use them, and the number of options can be overwhelming. Also, it can be tough to get the user experience right, when combining all of these options into one interface.

Fig 7.8: *In this system, no content is shown until after a user enters a search term or chooses a filter to use. Many more filters are available, providing more options.*

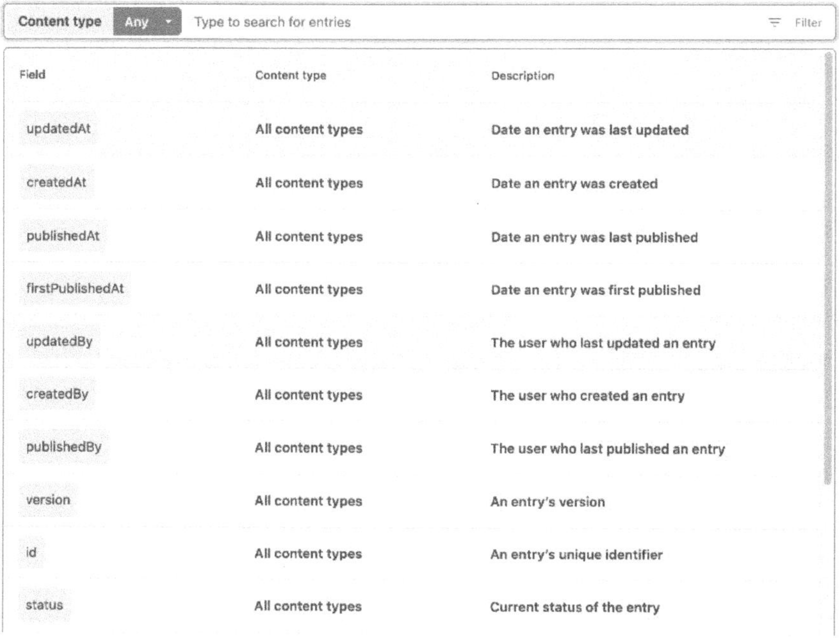

Content type Any Type to search for entries Filter

Field	Content type	Description
updatedAt	All content types	Date an entry was last updated
createdAt	All content types	Date an entry was created
publishedAt	All content types	Date an entry was last published
firstPublishedAt	All content types	Date an entry was first published
updatedBy	All content types	The user who last updated an entry
createdBy	All content types	The user who created an entry
publishedBy	All content types	The user who last published an entry
version	All content types	An entry's version
id	All content types	An entry's unique identifier
status	All content types	Current status of the entry

Fig 7.9: *A more advanced search interface can offer a wide variety of options, but at the expense of increased complexity.*

The more advanced interface in **Fig 7.9** is like the one in **Fig 7.8**, but it has several problems, which make it much less usable:

- There are too many options. Users see a long list, and it's not even the whole thing. More scrolling is needed.
- Many of these filters, like "id" and "version," are unlikely to be useful to everyday content authors. Others—such as variations on who created, edited, or published content and when—could be stripped down to a more manageable group.
- The filters use system language rather than human language. "publishedBy" and "articleBody" are the identifiers this system uses internally for content. These terms would be better replaced with plain language

like "Author" or "Article Text" so authors could search more effectively.

This kind of interface might be useful with a technical audience, but it's not going to serve most content authors well.

Mix and match

Regardless of your preference for content list vs. search, the main issue with any system-default content list is that it's not customized for your authors. The interfaces are designed to be generic and to work for the broadest possible audience. But, as we've seen throughout this book, there is no one solution to the problem of content findability. The best solution mixes these two paradigms. Start with a list of all content that authors can filter, then customize the filter options to match their needs (**Fig 7.10**).

If you have gone through a thorough research phase, you'll know the ways your authors use your system, and you can design search options and filters to help them do their jobs effectively.

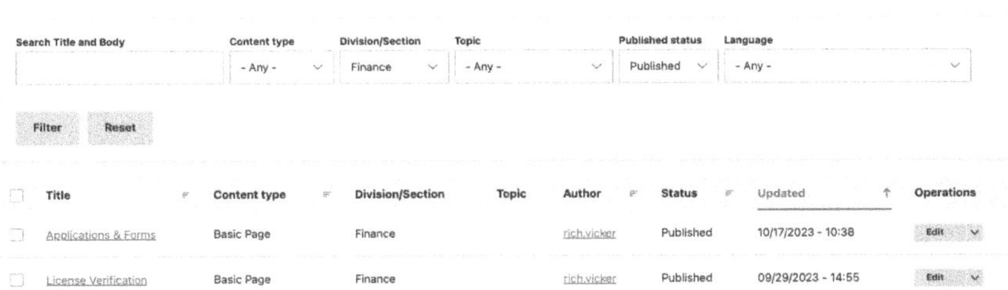

Fig 7.10: *This simple search and filtering interface for content authors includes a variety of filters that are useful for this client, such as Language, and eliminates others that are not.*

One size doesn't fit all

Content administration benefits from more context. Who are your authors? How familiar are they with the system? What are their roles? Understanding your authors allows you to build tools to support navigating the system and making the right content choices.

Now you know how to design forms and administrative tools to work for your authors. But is your new system accessible to everyone? Some authors manage content by using tools other than a browser and input devices other than a mouse. To serve these users, your system needs to follow authoring tool accessibility standards, which we'll discuss in the next chapter.

8. **Accessibility**

You hear a lot about website content accessibility but not as much about using accessibility principles to empower content authors do their jobs. Yet all kinds of people manage content and require some kind of accessibility accommodation.

Between 20 and 25% of the world's population has a permanent disability, many of which are invisible. Furthermore, anyone can have a temporary or situational disability, such as a broken arm. If your tools are not accessible, then you're not building for all content authors.

Accessibility standards

Accessibility standards for the web are set by the World Wide Web Consortium, more commonly referred to as the W3C. You may be familiar with the Web Content Accessibility Guidelines (WCAG) , which define levels of compliance to accessibility standards for web content. A second set of standards, called the Authoring Tool Accessibility Guidelines (ATAG) (*https://www.w3.org/WAI/standards-guidelines/atag/glance/*), defines compliance for tools that do things such as:

- Convert content, such as documents, into web formats
- Produce web content
- Create multimedia, such as photos and videos
- Manage the design and layout of web pages

Like WCAG, there are three conformance levels to ATAG 2.0: A, AA, and AAA. The ATAG standard has two areas of focus—making your authoring tools accessible (Part A), and making authoring tools that enable the creation of accessible content (Part B).

Use ATAG compliance as part of your criteria any time you evaluate a new CMS. You may find information related to ATAG in a vendor's Accessibility Conformance Report (ACR). However, out-of-the-box ATAG compliance won't help when you're building custom functionality. The more you can extend functionality that you already know is compliant, the less you have to worry about your own work being noncompliant.

It's impossible to get into the topic of accessibility in any real depth in a book of this length. Dive into the links in the Resources section if you're serious about how accessibility relates to the authoring experience, and want to explore the best solutions to these problems.

Making your authoring tool accessible

Part A of the ATAG standard defines how an authoring tool must be accessible. If you're familiar with the WCAG standards, you have a great foundation because most of the recommendations in Part A mirror accessibility practices for user-facing web content including the following:

- Images must have alternative text.
- Elements on the page should be structured properly.
- Components that exist across multiple pages must consistently appear in the same place.
- On-page text should be resizable without disrupting the page layout.

Hopefully your CMS is already built to meet these standards. Any custom functionality you have added should meet them as well.

Most authoring interfaces are more complex than the public-facing pages that they produce. An interface written in plain language, with clear online help available, is as important for accessibility as any of the functionality we'll discuss in the rest of this chapter. As we pointed out in the content entry chapter, you should use the language of your authors, and not the language of the CMS or developers who are implementing it.

Following WCAG standards will get you a long way towards ATAG compliance. However, given the complexity of most authoring systems, a few parts of the standard are worth closer attention.

Keyboard operation

WCAG requires that users can complete tasks using only the keyboard, since some users cannot use other input methods like a mouse. Screen-reader users on desktops are keyboard-only users, and some may use Bluetooth keyboards when navigating with their phones. Properly supporting keyboard use requires special attention, because many common author tasks are designed to be mouse-centric, such as these:

- Choosing a formatting button in a text editor
- Resizing table rows and columns
- Reordering items in a list via drag and drop
- Adding and moving components in a page builder

All of this functionality can work solely from the keyboard—if it's built the right way. For instance, screen-reader users can tab to an orderable list, have the list announce what position any item is in, and give instructions for how to reorder items using the keyboard.

Take these users into account when creating tools like this for your authoring system. It's easier to think about these issues during the design phase than it is to add them after the system has been completed.

Respecting preferences

Most modern operating systems and browsers have settings to enhance accessibility. Some users may need the ability to change color contrast settings, either to increase the contrast (for users who have trouble differentiating colors) or to decrease it (for users with dyslexia or light sensitivity). A user may also want to change their font size or default zoom level to make text more readable. Modern CSS media queries also allow users to set a preference for use of animation if they are affected by too much screen motion.

The authoring experience should respect a user's system-level changes and adapt appropriately. Users make these changes for good reasons, and ignoring them will make the authoring experience for them more difficult.

Accessible previews

Many authoring systems provide dynamic previews of content as it's created. Any previews must be as accessible as the content would be if it were rendered for an end user. That is, the HTML is properly structured, alternative text is included for non-text elements, the content is keyboard navigable, and so on. Everything you would do on the front-end should be done in your preview as well.

The purpose of a preview is for authors to understand how the content will be presented to end users when published. If a preview isn't accessible, authors using assistive devices will not be able to verify that the content is rendered as intended. Ideally, previews use the same templates and rendering engine that end users experience. Rendering the preview using the same HTML as the published page also allows more effective use of automated testing tools like Microsoft's Accessibility Insights (***https://accessibilityinsights.io/***) and the WebAIM WAVE Toolbar (***https://wave.webaim.org/extension/***).

Creating accessible content

Part B of ATAG defines different ways an authoring tool must support the creation of accessible content. This is the part of the authoring experience where the developer involved in designing the system probably has more control. There are many ways to encourage authors to create accessible content, but most of them are variations on one simple rule: Make doing the right thing easy and doing the wrong thing hard.

Authors are like anyone else—they do what's easy and quick. This is especially true for organizations with low content maturity, where authors may not understand the importance of accessible content to their audience and the organization. Authors must be able to create accessible content seamlessly, as a part of default workflows. Here are a few suggestions:

- Provide tools that enforce accessibility requirements, and turn them on by default. Most users should not have the option to turn them off.
- Offer documentation and training on authoring accessible content.
- Remove functionality such as HTML source code editing.

Some of these changes might not be popular with authors, as they remove flexibility and may increase the number of fields on forms. But creating accessible content is a legal requirement and a human imperative, and your authoring tool should ensure it.

Once again, this is a deep topic with lots of nuance. However, two areas worth special attention are images and alt text, and accessibility checkers. Let's look at those.

Images and alt text

Alternative text, or *alt text*, is a brief text description of an image that is read by assistive technology. Alt text provides context about the purpose of an image and its relationship to other page content. Authors must be able to add alt text to images they upload to the CMS. Here are some guidelines for supporting this functionality.

- **Require alt text.** Clients often ask me whether alt text should be a required field. Yes, it should. Requiring alt text encourages authors to create accessible content. When alt text isn't required, it's rarely entered. This is a failure for accessibility.
- **Help authors create alt text.** Provide direction so authors understand how to create meaningful alt text. Create documentation with examples of good alt text so authors can refer to it when they are uploading images.
- **Decorative images.** But what about decorative images, you say? Alt text on decorative images creates clutter for screen reader users, and it isn't required anyway. This is true, but most decorative images such as logos should be baked into your CMS templates. There's rarely a reason for authors to upload them. Avoid decorative images, and required alt text won't be a problem.

Accessibility checkers

Many modern systems include accessibility checkers. These tools identify accessibility problems and offer solutions. Different systems implement these tools in different ways, and they all have pros and cons. Choosing the best solution—or combination of solutions—will depend on your use case and your CMS.

Back-end checkers

The most common accessibility checker implementation is a button in a visual editor. When an author clicks the button, the tool reviews the content and reports the problems it finds. Authors can review and fix problems one by one (**Fig 8.1**).

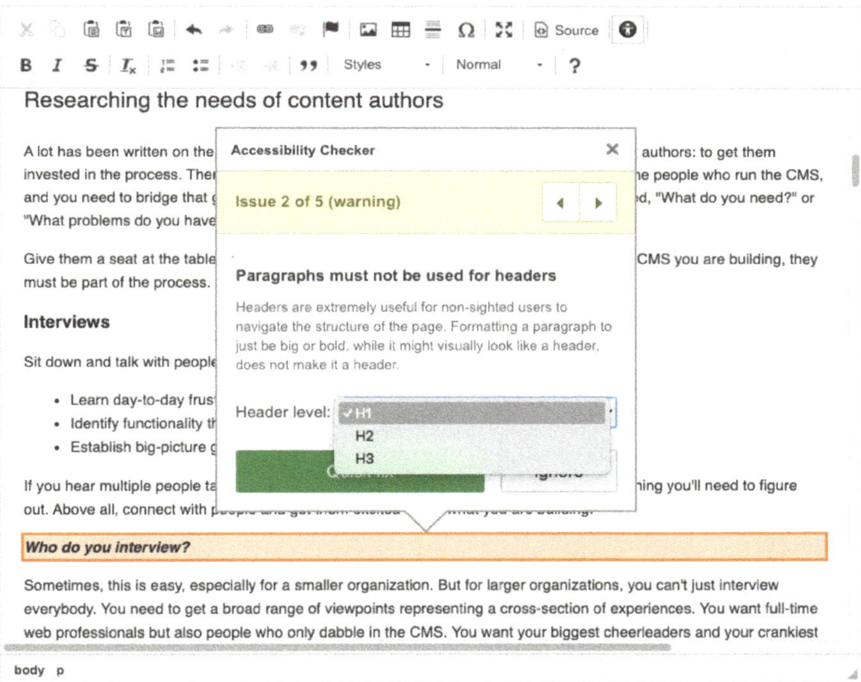

Fig 8.1: *Accessibility checkers built into visual editors can warn authors about issues, such as missing alt text and improperly formatted headers, and offer simple fixes.*

These tools are great for authors, and they're getting easier to use. Unfortunately, they require authors to click the button to get any useful information. If an author chooses not to use the checker, they may not know about the accessibility problems in their content.

Some tools have taken this a step further. A11yFirst (***https://a11yfirst.web.illinois.edu/***) is a plugin for the popular WYSIWYG editor, CKEditor . A11yFirst is designed to prevent accessibility issues from happening at all, rather than fixing them after the fact. For example, it has special code that keeps headings from being nested improperly. The program also requires that all images have alt text unless they are marked as decorative. In Chapter 6: Designing Forms, we learned how coercion (preventing errors) is generally preferred over validation (warning that an error has occurred)—and that's what's happening here. If you can prevent inaccessible content from being created, then you should.

Unfortunately, there's one problem with both of these solutions. They are attached to a visual editor and only scan the content that authors enter into that field. They don't catch accessibility problems that can happen in other fields. For instance, you might have an image upload field that doesn't ask for alt text. Or the field might require alt text but the template is built in such a way that the alt text isn't rendered. These tools won't identify those problems.

Front-end checkers

For a more complete picture of your accessibility problems, use a tool that scans the rendered page. This allows you to review the content as a whole, the way the user encounters it. A typical implementation of this kind of tool provides a warning for logged in users. It requires no author interaction to work—it just appears on every page as they're browsing. Authors can click the warning to see problems and solutions (**Fig 8.2**).

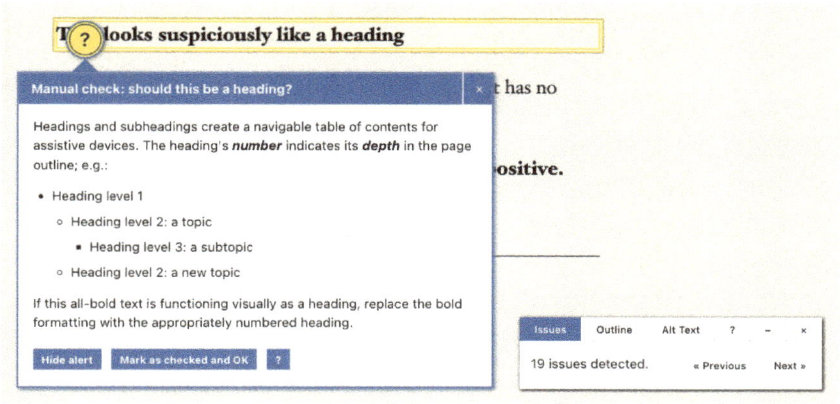

Fig 8.2: *The Editoria11y accessibility checker renders on the front end of a website, highlighting accessibility problems as authors browse.*

While front-end checkers offer a more complete view of accessibility issues, these tools don't offer an automated or easy way to fix the problems they find. An author has to leave the page they're on and go into the system's editing interface to make changes. This is more of a hassle and makes it less likely that any problems get fixed. These tools can also be distracting for authors who are trying to browse the site and read content themselves.

Back-end and front-end accessibility checkers aren't perfect, but either one is better than nothing and many organizations are starting to use some combination of both. As always, do your research and choose the tool that makes the most sense for your use case.

The best solution

The W3C plans to incorporate ATAG into the 3.0 update to WCAG. This means that regulations requiring WCAG compliance will include authoring tools as well. Now is a great time to look at your authoring tools and get a head start on bringing them into compliance.

We can create any number of tools to detect and fix inaccessible content, but nothing beats training and education. Authors can't find problems they don't understand, and they're more likely to fix issues they know are important to the organization. How do we communicate how the CMS works and what are the best solutions to common problems? And how do we support and empower authors to do their best work? That's what we'll discuss in our final chapter.

9. Support

The authoring experience isn't only about the screens authors interact with and the forms they fill out. It's also about the context for those actions—the organizational processes and culture that can either help or hinder authors when they use these tools.

That's where author support comes in. *Support* in this context refers to tools outside the CMS that enable authors to do their job. Support begins before the system is built and continues after it's launched. We'll discuss three common author support tools—copy decks, training, and documentation—and how each fits into the puzzle of creating a successful authoring experience.

Copy decks

A *copy deck* is a document that outlines the fields necessary to create a piece of content. Authors can use copy decks to collect all the required information before they enter content into the CMS. Copy decks are also useful early in a site build process, before a system is ready. They allow content authors to begin work on new site content before they have a live CMS. Once the CMS is ready to use, authors can use copy decks to guide content entry.

Copy decks have advantages over entering content straight into the CMS:

- **They're familiar.** Copy decks are usually Word or Google documents, which are familiar to most users. Unlike a specialized CMS administration interface, a document gives users the freedom to point and type. They can work though content in any order without worrying about validation or what content exists where.

- **They're collaborative.** Most organizations require some level of collaboration to create content, whether that means collecting assets, editing content someone else has written, or sending content for approval to other departments. A text-based document is better suited to this process than a CMS. A document is a writing and editing tool, and a CMS is a publishing tool. A document supports commenting, assigning tasks, and viewing past revisions. While some content management systems have these features, they are new and not areas that a CMS typically excels in. People have been using dedicated collaborative writing applications for over a decade. Sometimes the best solution for authors is to use the best tool for the job, and that tool is not always the CMS.

A well-designed copy deck (**Fig 9.1**) contains:

- The name of the content type.
- A description of the content. (What will it be used for? How does it fit, in relation to other content on the site?)
- The content's audience. (Who is the content for?)
- Content goals. (What does the audience expect to get from this content?)
- Actions you expect the audience to take. (What will the audience need to do?)
- A visual representation of the content as it will look when rendered on the site. (Will content authors have a difficult time thinking of content and fields in the abstract? A screen shot of the completed content or a link to a live example may help them visualize how the page comes together.)

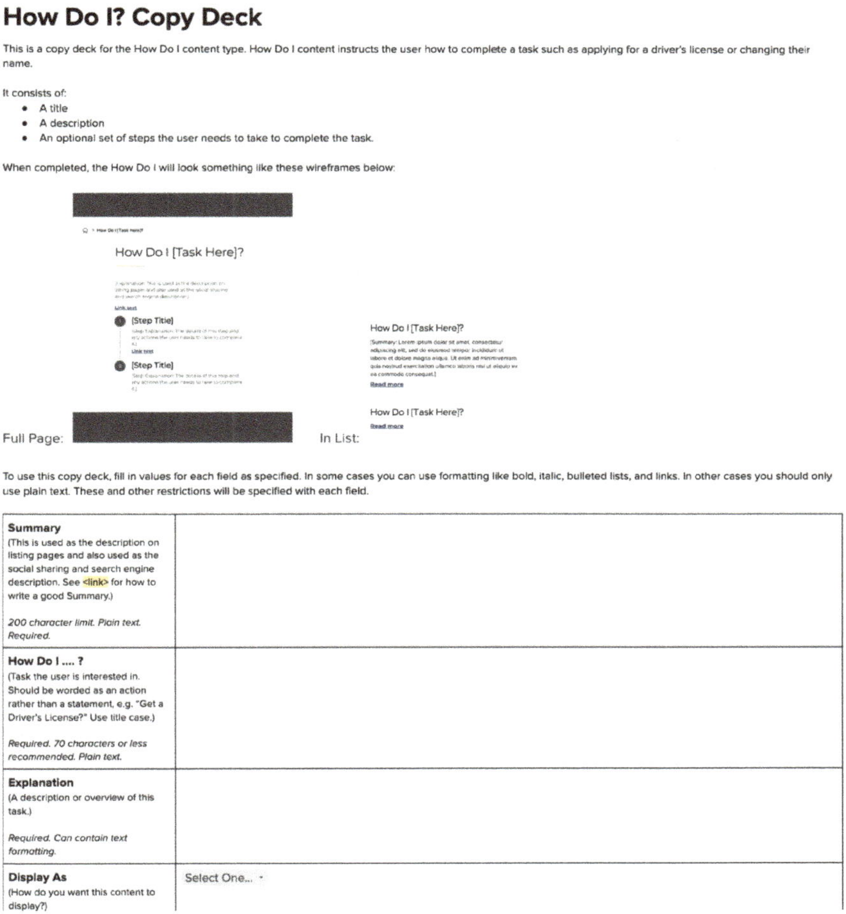

How Do I? Copy Deck

This is a copy deck for the How Do I content type. How Do I content instructs the user how to complete a task such as applying for a driver's license or changing their name.

It consists of:

- A title
- A description
- An optional set of steps the user needs to take to complete the task.

When completed, the How Do I will look something like these wireframes below:

To use this copy deck, fill in values for each field as specified. In some cases you can use formatting like bold, italic, bulleted lists, and links. In other cases you should only use plain text. These and other restrictions will be specified with each field.

Summary (This is used as the description on listing pages and also used as the social sharing and search engine description. See <link> for how to write a good Summary.) *200 character limit. Plain text. Required.*	
How Do I .... ? (Task the user is interested in. Should be worded as an action rather than a statement, e.g. "Get a Driver's License?" Use title case.) *Required. 70 characters or less recommended. Plain text.*	
Explanation (A description or overview of this task.) *Required. Can contain text formatting.*	
Display As (How do you want this content to display?)	Select One...

Fig 9.1: *This sample copy deck includes a description of the content type, a visual representation of the content to help ground authors, and places to fill in values for every field.*

Structure the copy deck as a table, with each row representing a field. In the left column, include the field's name, a description of its use, and any validation instructions. In the right column, include a space for authors to input their content.

In the instructions, provide links to documentation, style guides, or any other assets you have that support content creation. For example, authors might not understand meta descriptions, why they're important, or how to write a good one, but there are lots of resources out there that you can add to the field descriptions to help them learn.

For a complex content type with many fields, break the copy deck into sections to represent different parts of the page. This is a good technique for complex landing pages. Break them into distinct components, and give each section its own screenshot and set of fields to divide the page into parts.

For fields that allow multiple entries—such as a list of related products, links, or steps— switch to a horizontal table presentation. Make a new table and put the field descriptions across the top. Each cell below contains one instance of the property named above it (**Fig 9.2**).

Steps

Complete one row for each step as needed in your How Do I. There is no limit on how many steps you can have. A step should cover a single task. You should not merge multiple tasks into a single step. You do not have to have any Steps, they are optional. You can add as many steps as you need.

Title (Name of this step.) *Required. Plain text.*	**Explanation** (The details of this step and any actions the user needs to take to complete it.) *Required. Can contain text formatting.*	**URL** (A single call to action within the step. Where should the user start?) *Optional.*	**URL Text** (The text the user will click in order to browse to the URL.) *Required if a URL is provided.*

Fig 9.2: *Switch field descriptions from rows to columns, to include multiple instances of elements such as links or associated content.*

Creating a great authoring experience is not just form design. It also means giving authors the tools they need to solve problems. A well-designed copy deck will fit the bill for many tasks. Using a copy deck is also good practice for writing CMS help text and documentation. Because it includes the field names and supporting text for content entry, a copy deck can act as a test case. Does the help text make sense? Does it support authors in creating appropriate content? If it doesn't, this is a low-stakes way to adjust and make changes before the build.

At some point, however, authors will have to get content into the CMS. They'll have an easier job ahead of them if they have training and reference materials to guide them.

Training

Training provides instructional material for new users of a system to get them up and running. Writing a bunch of docs and putting them in Confluence is *not* training (although documentation is also useful and necessary, as we'll see). More than just teaching content authors how to use a CMS, training means teaching them how to do their jobs and meet their goals. Most people have some level of experience with web forms. Simply running through the form and its individual fields, and describing where to press save, does not bring a lot of value to your authors. Customize training to their needs and present it in a way they can digest.

Designing your training

It's not unusual for someone to deliver a generic course in "How to use <your CMS>" and leave it at that. But not all training is appropriate for all users. Design your training program to fit the needs of those who will be using it. (Seems like we've been saying that a lot, doesn't it?) Here are a few tips:

- **Adjust your training to fit your organization.** Training for a handful of content professionals in the marketing department at a startup will be different than training on a similar system for three PhD physicists at a university, or for 250 authors at an enterprise organization. Each group has different priorities, levels of CMS experience, and understandings of content and its place on the web.

- **Focus on the why.** Focus on the why of the system and let the what and how follow. Why would you pick one content type over another, and what are the implications of choosing improperly? Why is it important to create useful alternative text for images, and which users will be disenfranchised if you don't?
- **Consider roles and permissions.** In a system with role-based permissions, not all authors can perform all tasks. Some roles can only create content, while a smaller set of people might review and publish the content. Train these roles separately, or make it clear that not all functionality is available to everyone.

I've seen organizations have success with training that's designed around user journeys rather than a CMS walkthrough. Instead of "here are the content types and the fields on each one," you might have topics like these:

- Publicize a new research paper using the news content type.
- Create landing pages that drive traffic to different parts of your site.
- Communicate technical content to non-technical users.

Sometimes authors are left feeling confused after a training session, because they don't need to understand the CMS so much as they need to understand how to best get their job done. Build your training materials around this idea of helping authors do their best work.

Training delivery

The ideal type of training is delivered in real time by an expert who can explain well and also answer questions. Sessions can be in person or online, as long as the authors can access the system and someone is available for tech support in case of any problems.

Pre-recorded training has benefits, too—either as primary teaching material or as a supplement to real-time education. Recorded materials allow authors to work at their own pace, which is helpful for people who digest information slowly and risk getting left behind in a real-time class. Recorded materials also give people the opportunity to repeat sections. The downside is that trainees aren't able to ask questions, and questions often benefit the whole class, not only the person asking.

To ensure training is engaging and useful to your authors:

- **Show, don't tell.** *Show* authors how to use the system, providing examples that relate to their work instead of demonstrating different parts of the system and moving on.
- **Set up access in advance.** Give authors access to the system before the training, so they can follow along. Use a temporary sandbox, not the production website, so that authors can experiment without worrying that they will break anything. At an in-person training event, allow time for everyone joining virtually to log in, and make sure someone is available to work one-on-one with users experiencing technical issues.
- **Make it interactive.** Let content authors ask clarifying questions. Create a real-time communication channel, such as Slack, where people can get answers quickly. Post answers publicly, especially if the training is pre-recorded.
- **Guarantee accessibility.** Provide recordings of live trainings, including captions, after the meeting concludes.

Creating a useful, thoughtful training curriculum is a lot of work, and the less experienced your users are, the more work—and the more necessary—it will be. Proper training produces comfortable and confident site authors—and that means better content.

Documentation

If training is for new users, then documentation is for existing users. Documentation is primarily a reference, targeted to give people familiar with the system a place to find answers to questions or refresh themselves on how things work.

Documentation goals are different from training goals. With documentation, you want to:

- **Focus on what and how.** Training covers *why*, while documentation emphasizes *what* and *how*. *What* is the testimonail content type? What fields are included, and what are their parameters? Documentation provides detailed answers to these questions.
- **Write it down.** While training is best in video format, documentation is best when it's written. Well-organized, written documentation helps authors quickly find things while ignoring the surrounding material.
- **Use visual examples.** Provide examples of display variations in your documentation. A CMS may have fields that change the way a component displays on the screen. For example, the author may choose whether an image displays on the left or right side of a screen. In your documentation, you can show how this will look, side by side along with a field's details. Authors will see how a change might impact the content's presentation. You can also present different views; for instance, how a content type displays at medium or small screen resolutions.

There are several ways you can create and organize documentation. Let's explore some of them.

Types of documentation

Documentation is most commonly hosted on a dedicated website. There are as many ways to build a documentation site as there are stars in the sky. This might be why teams spend way too much time on tooling and not enough time worrying about content. Use the tools you have to document what you've built.

It may seem odd in our digital era, but printed references can also be useful. A university client I worked with had made a quick reference guide for their CMS, showing the content components available on their landing pages as well as their layout variations (**Fig 9.3**). Some content authors printed it out and hung it on their walls, because sometimes a glance is all you need to remember how something works. The team considered this documentation to be as much of a success as their web-based technical documentation, and they later expanded it.

What to include

Documentation should be written in plain language and have complete coverage of the system. This should include (but not be limited to) the following:

- Available content types
- Fields and attributes
- Content creation best practices
- Writing guidelines
- Workflow specifications
- Roles and permissions

Fig 9.3: *Quick reference guides can show a lot of information in a small amount of space, using visuals that editors can easily understand.*

A government client we worked with also did more than write a bunch of words when they designed their documentation. They took screenshots of the editorial interface, labeled each field, and showed where that field appears on the page and what it looks like (**Fig 9.4**). This helped to translate an abstract concept (a form) into something concrete (a web page). The downside is that screenshots are a lot of work to update when your CMS changes. If you go this route, plan for future maintenance of screen shots in addition to text updates.

Authors need advice about how to use the CMS and how to create good content. The best documentation is a combination of technical manual and writing guide, covering topics like voice and tone, writing style, and accessibility.

Documentation is *not* a substitute for training. Many organizations create documentation and dump new users into the pool hoping they can figure out how to swim. Training provides initial knowledge and context that authors need in order to get oriented and experienced within a system. Documentation serves as backup and support for them as they continue in their roles.

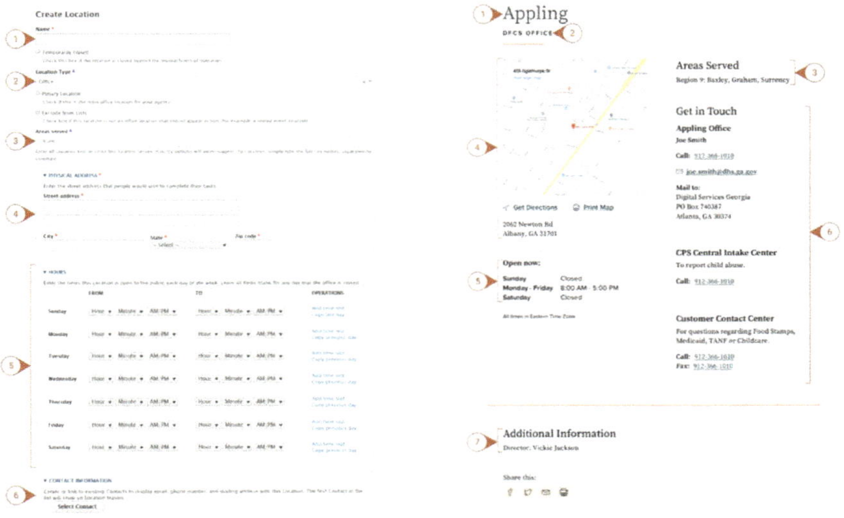

9.4: *Screenshots comparing the editorial interface and website front end can turn documentation from text on a screen into something more functional.*

Care and pruning

Your CMS is a site of growth and change, and that means providing authors with ongoing support. Without maintenance and continuing education, even a well-made system can wither. Here are a few best practices for content maintenance:

- **Update documentation.** Systems change over time. Reflect those changes in your documentation. Track new releases and get the documentation updated. Out-of-date documentation isn't a technical problem but a human one. There's only one way to make sure updates happen—create a process and put someone in charge of following it.

- **Create communities of practice.** Get your content authors working together and learning from each other. You can simply schedule "lunch and learn" sessions, or plan something more involved. The State of Georgia has a semi-annual conference called GovTalks (***https://digital.georgia.gov/govtalks***) where authors from the state's agencies learn about updates and improvements to their systems, what's working at other states, and general technology trends. When authors build community, it creates a culture of skill development and progress, and results in better content for audiences.
- **Support continuing education.** The technology of your CMS isn't the only thing that changes. Web and internet technology constantly change as well. That's not something you can document, but you can offer continuing education. Keep authors invested in their work by providing ways for them to learn and grow. Many conferences make their recorded talks available to the public. Share them with your site authors when they're interesting and relevant.
- **Gather feedback.** For formal author support requests, use a bug tracking or ticketing system. This kind of software lets authors track the progress of their requests and get notified when they have been resolved.

Don't make the mistake of thinking your work is done once your system is launched. Your CMS—and its content and authors—are like a garden that requires care over time so it doesn't become tangled and overgrown.

More than the CMS

One of the themes of this book is that the authoring experience goes well past the confines of the CMS. To make a great product, you have to learn who your authors are, understand the context of their work, and support their efforts and growth. That support most often takes the form of documentation and training. Ongoing support will also ensure the CMS grows and provides help to authors when they encounter problems or request missing functionality. Support is part of success.

Conclusion

You may be thinking to yourself, "Wow! This is like an entire second web project in parallel to the main one!" Well, you're right. There's no way around it. Your content authors are users just like your site visitors, and they deserve the same processes and attention.

In short, by following what's outlined in this book, you will:

- Design a CMS that supports content authors as much as it supports your organization.
- Learn about the context your authors work in.
- Learn the importance of talking to them and understanding their needs.
- Be able to verify your ideas.
- Know how to build a more user-friendly content management system.
- Know how to ensure your CMS is accessible.
- Learn the value of providing support with training and documentation.

Improving the authoring experience means focusing on authors, and you can't do that without involving them in the process. Always build your system with authors' needs in mind. Everything else branches out from that one principle.

I hope you've come out of reading this book ready to change the world—or at least ready to make life better for content authors. Maybe two or three things here feel particularly applicable to your own situation. Try them out!

Go talk to some content authors. Get involved in planning for your next set of CMS features. Start a community of practice with your authoring team by meeting regularly to talk about how to produce better content and to discuss the general state of the web.

Soon you'll find these small things start to pay off, and bigger initiatives will spawn from them. Keep moving that needle forward and you'll make life better for all your authors along the way. Best of luck!

Acknowledgments

In 2022 I was rolling off a large-scale CMS implementation project, and my mind was buzzing with ideas that couldn't seem to find their way out. I had been involved in several projects in a row that struggled with similar problems around content governance, organizational conflict, authors who were frustrated, and content that was subpar. Finally, I sat down with a whiteboard to figure out how I could tie all these ideas together and what the output of that would be. A series of articles? A talk? Well, it turned out to be all of those things, but one thing that really grabbed me was the idea of taking my work on the content authoring experience and sharing it with the world. Soon after, I wrote a book pitch and sent it to my dream publisher, A Book Apart—and to my great shock they said yes.

I spent the last six months of 2022 writing the first draft of this book. Just as I began my first round of revisions, I received notice that A Book Apart was pausing all books currently in process, with the intention of restarting them within a few months. Sadly, that never occurred, and in July 2023, my book (and every other ABA book in progress) was cancelled. I approached several other publishers but couldn't find anyone interested. So finally, in early 2024, I launched a Kickstarter campaign to complete this book—and to my utter and complete astonishment, I managed to raise the funds needed to pay for the editing, design, and production of the book you now hold in your hands.

While it didn't go as planned, I am very grateful to Katel LeDû and Lisa Maria Marquis at A Book Apart for believing in this book and giving me the kick I needed to get it off the ground. My wife Nicole was endlessly supportive of this endeavor from the very beginning. She gave me the space to write and edit and fret and pace through an interstate move and a number of other life crises. I am so thankful to her and our furry family for their support and confidence.

A huge thank you to my editorial and production collaborators on this finished product. Frances Duncan patiently suffered through multiple rounds of developmental edit, providing crucial feedback on many of the book's thorniest problems. I would not have made it through that process without her. Susan Bond provided a much-needed copyedit on a tight timeline, making the book exponentially more readable. Brenda Halvorson shepherded me through production and design, helping me choose fonts and create all the formats needed for both print and digital. Her experience and skill would have taken me another year to figure out by myself.

Anything I've accomplished professionally in the past decade would not have been possible without the collaboration of my colleagues at Lullabot, whose dedication and craft are without parallel in my 30 years of professional experience. Many of the documents, designs, and other artifacts cited in this book are a result of that collaboration, so credit is due to the people whose input and support were critical to those projects' success: Andrew Berry, Seth Brown, Marcos Cano, Jeff Eaton, Marissa Epstein, Nikki Flores, Stephanie Ganzer, Matt Kleve, Darren Peterson, Megh Plunkett, Jared Ponchot, Erin Schroeder, Kat Shaw, Brian Skowron, Hawkeye Tenderwolf, Jen Witkowski, Sally Young, and anyone else I inevitably failed to mention.

One of my first CMS projects was in 2006, at The Seattle Times, where I merged a hodge podge of custom-built systems into a single cohesive one. After that project launched, one of the content authors reached out to me, asking where an indispensable piece of functionality was. After talking to them a bit, I realized that it had never been built. And the reason it had never been built was that throughout the entire project, we had never talked to the authors about the work they were doing and what they needed. This was the first ever spark that got me thinking about content authors and their place in the process. The crew I worked with at The Seattle Times was incredible, creative, and inspiring. Thank you to Geoff Carter, Sean Carberry, Monica Fischer, Gary Love, John Palmer, Sheri Quirt, and Neal Schindler for kicking this all off.

This book also wouldn't exist without the collaborators our team had when working on the GovHub platform for the state of Georgia. Thank you to Nikhil Deshpande, Jasmyne Epps, Rachel Hart, Donna Sumner, and everyone else on the Digital Services team for giving us the chance to focus on content authors as primary users in their project.

Thank you to Mike Gifford for his extremely helpful review and comments on the Accessibility chapter. Andrew Berry and Frances Duncan also provided early feedback integral to the book's success.

Thanks to Michael Wilson for helping me resurrect MADMIN, the first CMS I ever wrote.

Finally, thank you to everyone who supported my Kickstarter campaign. I don't even know where to begin. If you shared a post, or promoted the campaign to social, or even liked a post or sent a message of support, then you were part of this project's success. The following people pledged more than $50 to the campaign, and their contributions are the only reason this book exists at all. Thank you all, from the bottom of my heart.

Scott Abel ☆ Acolono
☆ Trent Augenstein ☆ Johannes Baas ☆ Nic Barajas ☆
Deane Barker ☆ Donna Benjamin ☆ Andrew Berry
☆ Jerad Bitner ☆ Alisa Bonsignore ☆ Janus Boye ☆
Karen Brothers ☆ Kit Brown ☆ Seth Brown ☆ James Callan
☆ Dachary Carey ☆ Dulce Carrillo ☆ Anita Cheng ☆
Pei Chien ☆ Chris Coyier ☆ Sarah Maxell Crosby ☆ Orin Day
☆ Jaydee Devine ☆ April Duangjumpa ☆ Frances Duncan ☆
Penni Epstein ☆ Gavin Estey ☆ Ellie Fanning
☆ Nikki Flores ☆ Micheal Foley ☆ Stephanie Ganzer ☆
Anne Gibson ☆ Mike Gifford ☆ Casey Gollan ☆ Jason Grigsby
☆ Christi Guzik ☆ Kristina Halvorson ☆ Carrie Hane ☆
Laura Herring ☆ Ben Higgins ☆ David Hobbs
☆ Sarah Hopkins ☆ Jenna ☆ Simon R Jones ☆
Shelley Keith ☆ Bálint Kléri ☆ Kris Konrady
☆ Paul Kruczynski ☆ Paula Land ☆ Shannon Leahy ☆
Katel LeDû ☆ Mark Llobrera ☆ Alexis Logsdon
☆ Rachel Lovinger ☆ Keisha M ☆ Lisa Maria Marquis ☆
Amber Matz ☆ Karen McGrane ☆ Claire McSherry
☆ Melinda Miller ☆ Michal Minecki ☆
Lisa Mirabile ☆ McGee Noble ☆ Sarah O'Keefe
☆ Matthew Oliveira ☆ Andrew Parrucci ☆ Steve Persch ☆
Darren Petersen ☆ Mike Powers ☆ Randy (Amazing Rando)
☆ Dave Reid ☆ Aubrey Sambor ☆ Echa Schneider ☆
Erin Schroeder ☆ Brian Skowron ☆ Robin Smail
☆ Akshay Sura ☆ Larry Swanson ☆ Sarah Thrasher ☆
J.J. Toothman ☆ Kurt Trowbridge ☆ Tom Uban
☆ Ariel Van Spronsen ☆ Kristof Van Tomme ☆ John VanDyk ☆
Adam Varn ☆ Corey Vilhauer ☆ Brian Wallace
☆ Sean Walsh ☆ Katy Watkins ☆ Eileen Webb ☆
Andy Welfle ☆ Amy Wells ☆ Wendell
☆ Dylan Wilbanks ☆ Daniel Williams ☆ Morgan Williams ☆
Lynn Winter ☆ Cordelia Yu ☆ Karen Ziv ★

Resources

I have made the screenshots, links, and resources used in this book available online for easier use. Feel free to visit *https://authoringexperience.com/resources* or scan the QR code to access them.

The Authoring Experience

- Web Content Management: Systems, Features, and Best Practices by Deane Barker (*https://deanebarker.net/books/squirrel/*)
- The Web Project Guide by Corey Vilhauer and Deane Barker (*https://webproject.guide/*)

Structure vs. Flexibility

- "Real World Content Modeling" by Deane Barker (*https://deanebarker.net/books/real-world-content-modeling/*)
- Designing Connected Content: Plan and Model Digital Products for Today and Tomorrow by Mike Atherton and Carrie Hane (*https://www.pearson.com/en-us/subject-catalog/p/designing-connected-content-plan-and-model-digital-products-for-today-and-tomorrow/P200000009416/9780134763385*)
- "Page Builders vs. Traditional CMS" – an episode of the Cutting Edge Web Development podcast, featuring Jeff Eaton and Karen McGrane (*https://www.youtube.com/watch?v=xhVmvsUQGwQ*)

Understanding Your Organization

- There are various models to understand phases of content maturity, but I like this one from Content Strategy Inc. (*https://contentstrategyinc.com/understanding-content-maturity-model/*)

Understanding Your Authors

- Just Enough Research by Erika Hall (*https://abookapart.com/products/just-enough-research*)
- 18F Methods is a collection of tools and exercises that can be used to gather information from users and identify needs for a digital project. (*https://guides.18f.gov/methods/*)

Prototyping

- Nu Board portable white boards (*https://www.amazon.com/stores/nu+board/page/9A80A51B-49F8-46D2-B28C-0655AF5096F9?ref_=ast_bln*)
- Optimal Workshop is a popular tool for doing click-testing as well as other types of user testing. (*https://www.optimalworkshop.com/product/first-click-testing*)

Designing Forms

- *Forms That Work: Designing Web Forms for Usability* by Steve Kruger, Caroline Jarrett, and Gerry Gaffney (*https://www.elsevier.com/books/forms-that-work/krug/978-1-55860-710-1*)
- *Form Design Patterns* by Adam Silver (*https://formdesignpatterns.com/*). Adam also has an excellent newsletter that often talks about form design, which you can sign up for at (*https://adamsilver.io/*)

- *Designing UX: Forms* by Jessica Enders (***https://www.sitepoint.com/premium/books/designing-ux-forms/***)
- Federal Plain Language Guidelines (***https://www.plainlanguage.gov/guidelines/***)
- Center for Plain Language (***https://centerforplainlanguage.org/***)
- "6 Ways to Reduce Cognitive Load for a Better UI" by Vitor Guerra (***https://xd.adobe.com/ideas/process/information-architecture/6-ways-to-reduce-cognitive-load-for-a-better-ui/***)
- "Exploring the Gestalt Principles of Design" by Cameron Chapman (***https://www.toptal.com/designers/ui/gestalt-principles-of-design***)
- "How to Provide Accessible Form Error Identification" by Level Access (***https://www.levelaccess.com/level-access-news/how-to-provide-accessible-error-identification/***)

Content Administration

- The interface for choosing a content type was developed by Lullabot for the state of Georgia. It was released as a freely downloadable module for Drupal called Type Tray (***https://drupal.org/project/type_tray***), and you can read more about it on the state's website (***https://digital.georgia.gov/hub/2021-03-04/type-tray***).

Accessibility

- "4 Major Patterns for Accessible Drag and Drop" by Jesse Hausler (***https://medium.com/salesforce-ux/4-major-patterns-for-accessible-drag-and-drop-1d43f64ebf09***)
- We 4 Authors Cluster
  This was a pilot podcast on web accessibility for web authoring tools producers and communities led by

Funka, a Swedish agency specializing in accessibility services. This playlist shows examples of how different authoring tasks could be made more accessible. (*https://www.youtube.com/playlist?list=PLnZ9mijo8V_DuYDRAvMlaTUeNgiwcBXaD*)

- "Introduction to Web Accessibility"
  W3C offers a free online digital accessibility foundations course. (*https://www.w3.org/WAI/courses/foundations-course/*)
- "Accessibility for Content Designers"
  The General Services Administration created a quick-start guide for embedding accessibility and inclusive design practices into your team's workflow that offers a lot of useful high-level tips for designers and developers. (*https://digital.gov/guides/accessibility-for-teams/content-design/#content-start*)

Support

- *Leading Content Design* by Rachel McConnell (*https://www.rachelmcconnell.me/leadingcontentdesign*)
- *From Solo to Scaled: Building a Sustainable Content Strategy Practice* by Natalie Marie Dunbar (*https://rosenfeldmedia.com/books/from-solo-to-scaled-building-a-sustainable-content-strategy-practice/*)

About the Author

Greg Dunlap got started in content management in the early 2000s, building custom systems for small clients. In 2006 at the Seattle Times Company, Greg got involved in the Drupal community, eventually leading one of the eight core initiatives for Drupal 8. Since then he has focused on building large-scale publishing systems for clients around the world.

Greg makes his home in rural Washington with his wife Nicole and a small menagerie of animal friends. In his spare time, Greg is an internationally ranked pinball player and loud-music concert goer.

The color of this book was inspired by the fur under the chin of my cat Ozu, who we lost several years ago. Miss you, buddy.

www.ingramcontent.com/pod-product-compliance
Ingram Content Group UK Ltd.
Pitfield, Milton Keynes, MK11 3LW, UK
UKHW050716100225
4517UKWH00047B/598

9 798991 762908